Blue Ocean Strategy

Blue Ocean Strategy

How to Create Uncontested Market Space and

Make the Competition Irrelevant

W. Chan Kim

Renée Mauborgne

HARVARD BUSINESS SCHOOL PRESS

BOSTON, MASSACHUSETTS

978-1-59139-619-2 (ISBN 13)

Library of Congress Cataloging-in-Publication Data

Kim, W. Chan.
    Blue ocean strategy: how to create uncontested market space and make the
    competition irrelevant / W. Chan Kim, Renée Mauborgne.
        p.   cm.
    Includes bibliographical references and index.
    ISBN 1-59139-619-0 (hardcover: alk. paper)
    1. New products. 2. Market segmentation. I. Mauborgne, Renée. II. Title.
    HF5415.153.K53   2005
    658.8'02—dc22

                                                                    2004020857

The paper used in this publication meets the requirements of the American National
Standard for Permanence of Paper for Publications and Documents in Libraries and
Archives Z39.48–1992

To friendship and to our families,

who make our worlds

more meaningful

Contents

Part Three: Executing Blue Ocean Strategy

Preface

THIS IS A BOOK about friendship, about loyalty, about believing in one another. It was because of that friendship, and that belief, that we set out on the journey to explore the ideas in this book and eventually came to write it.

We met twenty years ago in a classroom—one the professor, the other the student. And we have worked together ever since, often seeing ourselves along the journey as two wet rats in a drain. This book is not the victory of an idea but of a friendship that we have found more meaningful than any idea in the world of business. It has made our lives rich and our worlds more beautiful. We were not alone.

No journey is easy; no friendship is filled only with laughter. But we were excited every day of that journey because we were on a mission to learn and improve. We believe passionately in the ideas in this book. These ideas are not for those whose ambition in life is to get by or merely to survive. That was never an interest of ours. If you can be satisfied with that, do not read on. But if you want to make a difference, to create a company that builds a future where customers, employees, shareholders, and society win, read on. We are not saying it is easy, but it is worthwhile.

Our research confirms that there are no permanently excellent companies, just as there are no permanently excellent industries. As we have found on our own tumbling road, we all, like corporations, do smart things and less-than-smart things. To improve the quality of our success we need to study what we did that made a positive difference and understand how to replicate it systematically. That is what we call making smart strategic moves, and we have found that the strategic move that matters centrally is to create blue oceans.

Blue ocean strategy challenges companies to break out of the red ocean of bloody competition by creating uncontested market space that makes the competition irrelevant. Instead of dividing up existing—and often shrinking—demand and benchmarking competitors, blue ocean strategy is about growing demand and breaking away from the competition. This book not only challenges companies but also shows them how to achieve this. We first introduce a set of analytical tools and frameworks that show you how to systematically act on this challenge, and, second, we elaborate the principles that define and separate blue ocean strategy from competition-based strategic thought.

Our aim is to make the formulation and execution of blue ocean strategy as systematic and actionable as competing in the red waters of known market space. Only then can companies step up to the challenge of creating blue oceans in a smart and responsible way that is both opportunity maximizing and risk minimizing. No company—large or small, incumbent or new entrant—can afford to be a riverboat gambler. And no company should.

The contents of this book are based on more than fifteen years of research, data stretching back more than a hundred years, and a series of *Harvard Business Review* articles as well as academic articles on various dimensions of this topic. The ideas, tools, and frameworks presented here have been further tested and refined over the years in corporate practice in Europe, the United States, and Asia. This book builds on and extends this work by providing a narrative arc that draws these ideas together to offer a unified framework. This framework addresses not only the analytic aspects behind the creation of blue ocean strategy but also the all-important human aspects of how to bring an organization and its people on this journey with a willingness to execute these ideas in action. Here, understanding how to build trust and commitment, as well as an understanding of the importance of intellectual and emotional recognition, are highlighted and brought to the core of strategy.

Blue ocean opportunities have been out there. As they have been explored, the market universe has been expanding. This expansion, we believe, is the root of growth. Yet poor understanding exists both in theory and in practice as to how to systematically create and capture blue oceans. We invite you to read this book to learn how you can be a driver of this expansion in the future.

Acknowledgments

W E HAVE HAD SIGNIFICANT HELP in actualizing this book. INSEAD has provided a unique environment in which to conduct our research. We have benefited greatly from the crossover between theory and practice that exists at INSEAD, and from the truly global composition of our faculty, student, and executive education populations. Deans Antonio Borges, Gabriel Hawawini, and Ludo Van der Heyden provided encouragement and institutional support from the start and allowed us to closely intertwine our research and teaching. Pricewaterhouse-Coopers (PwC) and the Boston Consulting Group (BCG) have extended the financial support for our research; in particular, Frank Brown and Richard Baird at PwC, and René Abate, John Clarkeson, George Stalk, and Olivier Tardy of BCG have been valued partners.

While we had help from a highly talented group of researchers over the years, our two dedicated research associates, Jason Hunter and Ji Mi, who have worked with us for the last several years, deserve special mention. Their commitment, persistent research support, and drive for perfection, were essential in realizing this book. We feel blessed by their presence.

Our colleagues at the school have contributed to the ideas in the book. INSEAD faculty members, particularly Subramanian Rangan and Ludo Van der Heyden, helped us to reflect upon our ideas and offered valuable comments and support. Many of INSEAD's faculty have taught the ideas and frameworks in this book to executive and M.B.A. audiences, providing valuable feedback that sharpened our thinking. Others have provided intellectual encouragement and the energy of kindness. We thank here, among others, Ron Adner, Jean-Louis Barsoux, Ben Bensaou, Henri-Claude de Bettignies, Mike Brimm, Laurence Capron, Marco Ceccagnoli, Karel Cool, Arnoud De Meyer, Ingemar Dierickx, Gareth Dyas, George Eapen, Paul Evans, Charlie Galunic, Annabelle Gawer, Javier Gimeno, Dominique Héau, Neil Jones, Philippe Lasserre, Jean-François Manzoni, Jens Meyer, Claude Michaud, Deigan Morris, Quy Nguyen-Huy, Subramanian Rangan, Jonathan Story, Heinz Thanheiser, Ludo Van der Heyden, David Young, Peter Zemsky, and Ming Zeng.

We have been fortunate to have a network of practitioners and case writers across the globe. They have contributed greatly in showing how the ideas in this book apply in action and helping to develop case material for our research. Among many people, one deserves special mention: Marc Beauvois-Coladon, who has worked with us from the start and made a major contribution to chapter 4 based on his field experiences practicing our ideas in companies. Among the wealth of others, we would like to thank Francis Gouillart and his associates; Gavin Fraser and his associates; Wayne Mortensen; Brian Marks; Kenneth Lau; Yasushi Shiina; Jonathan Landrey and his associates; Junan Jiang; Ralph Trombetta and his associates; Gabor Burt and his associates; Shantaram Venkatesh; Miki Kawawa and her associates; Atul Sinha and his associates; Arnold Izsak and his associates; Volker Westermann and his associates; Matt Williamson; and Caroline Edwards and her associates. We also appreciate the emerging cooperation with Accenture as kicked off with Mark Spelman, Omar Abbosh, Jim Sayles, and their team. Thanks are also due to Lucent Technologies for their support.

During the course of our research, we have met with corporate executives and public officers around the world who generously gave us their time and insight, greatly shaping the ideas in this book. We are grateful to them. Among many private and public initiatives for putting our ideas into practice, the Value Innovation Program (VIP) Center at Samsung Electronics and the Value Innovation Action Tank (VIAT) in Singapore for the country's government and private sectors have been major sources of inspiration and learning. In particular, Jong-Yong Yun at Samsung Electronics and all the Permanent Secretaries of Singapore Government have been valued partners. Warm thanks also to the members of the Value Innovation Network (VIN), a global community of practice on the Value Innovation family of concepts—especially to those we were unable to mention here.

Finally, we would like to thank Melinda Merino, our editor, for her wise comments and editorial feedback, and the Harvard Business School Publishing team for their commitment and enthusiastic support. Thanks also to our present and past editors at *Harvard Business Review,* in particular David Champion, Tom Stewart, Nan Stone, and Joan Magretta. We owe a great deal to INSEAD M.B.A.'s and Ph.D.'s and executive education participants. Particularly, participants in both Strategy and Value Innovation Study Group (VISG) courses have been patient as we have tried out the ideas in this book. Their challenging questions and thoughtful feedback clarified and strengthened our ideas.

PART ONE

Blue Ocean Strategy

CHAPTER 1

Creating Blue Oceans

A ONE TIME ACCORDION PLAYER, stilt-walker, and fire-
eater, Guy Laliberté is now CEO of Cirque du Soleil,
one of Canada's largest cultural exports. Created in 1984 by a group
of street performers, Cirque's productions have been seen by almost
forty million people in ninety cities around the world. In less than
twenty years Cirque du Soleil has achieved a level of revenues that
took Ringling Bros. and Barnum & Bailey—the global champion of
the circus industry—more than one hundred years to attain.

What makes this rapid growth all the more remarkable is that it
was not achieved in an attractive industry but rather in a declining
industry in which traditional strategic analysis pointed to limited
potential for growth. Supplier power on the part of star performers
was strong. So was buyer power. Alternative forms of entertainment—ranging from various kinds of urban live entertainment to
sporting events to home entertainment—cast an increasingly long
shadow. Children cried out for PlayStations rather than a visit to
the traveling circus. Partially as a result, the industry was suffer-
ing from steadily decreasing audiences and, in turn, declining revenue and profits. There was also increasing sentiment against the

use of animals in circuses by animal rights groups. Ringling Bros. and Barnum & Bailey set the standard, and competing smaller circuses essentially followed with scaled-down versions. From the perspective of competition-based strategy, then, the circus industry appeared unattractive.

Another compelling aspect of Cirque du Soleil's success is that it did not win by taking customers from the already shrinking circus industry, which historically catered to children. Cirque du Soleil did not compete with Ringling Bros. and Barnum & Bailey. Instead it created uncontested new market space that made the competition irrelevant. It appealed to a whole new group of customers: adults and corporate clients prepared to pay a price several times as great as traditional circuses for an unprecedented entertainment experience. Significantly, one of the first Cirque productions was titled "We Reinvent the Circus."

New Market Space

Cirque du Soleil succeeded because it realized that to win in the future, companies must stop competing with each other. The only way to beat the competition is to stop *trying* to beat the competition.

To understand what Cirque du Soleil has achieved, imagine a market universe composed of two sorts of oceans: red oceans and blue oceans. Red oceans represent all the industries in existence today. This is the known market space. Blue oceans denote all the industries *not* in existence today. This is the unknown market space.

In the red oceans, industry boundaries are defined and accepted, and the competitive rules of the game are known.[1] Here, companies try to outperform their rivals to grab a greater share of existing demand. As the market space gets crowded, prospects for profits and growth are reduced. Products become commodities, and cutthroat competition turns the red ocean bloody.

Blue oceans, in contrast, are defined by untapped market space, demand creation, and the opportunity for highly profitable growth.

Although some blue oceans are created well beyond existing industry boundaries, most are created from within red oceans by expanding existing industry boundaries, as Cirque du Soleil did. In blue oceans, competition is irrelevant because the rules of the game are waiting to be set.

It will always be important to swim successfully in the red ocean by outcompeting rivals. Red oceans will always matter and will always be a fact of business life. But with supply exceeding demand in more industries, competing for a share of contracting markets, while necessary, will not be sufficient to sustain high performance.[2] Companies need to go beyond competing. To seize new profit and growth opportunities, they also need to create blue oceans.

Unfortunately, blue oceans are largely uncharted. The dominant focus of strategy work over the past twenty-five years has been on competition-based red ocean strategies.[3] The result has been a fairly good understanding of how to compete skillfully in red waters, from analyzing the underlying economic structure of an existing industry, to choosing a strategic position of low cost or differentiation or focus, to benchmarking the competition. Some discussions around blue oceans exist.[4] However, there is little practical guidance on how to create them. Without analytic frameworks to create blue oceans and principles to effectively manage risk, creating blue oceans has remained wishful thinking that is seen as too risky for managers to pursue as strategy. This book provides practical frameworks and analytics for the systematic pursuit and capture of blue oceans.

The Continuing Creation of Blue Oceans

Although the term *blue oceans* is new, their existence is not. They are a feature of business life, past and present. Look back one hundred years and ask yourself, How many of today's industries were then unknown? The answer: Many industries as basic as automobiles, music recording, aviation, petrochemicals, health care, and management consulting were unheard of or had just begun to emerge at that time. Now turn the clock back only thirty years. Again, a plethora of multibillion-dollar industries jumps out—mutual funds, cell phones, gas-fired electricity plants, biotechnology, discount retail, express package delivery, minivans, snowboards, coffee bars, and home videos, to name a few. Just three decades ago, none of these industries existed in a meaningful way.

Now put the clock forward twenty years—or perhaps fifty years— and ask yourself how many now unknown industries will likely exist then. If history is any predictor of the future, again the answer is many of them.

The reality is that industries never stand still. They continuously evolve. Operations improve, markets expand, and players come and go. History teaches us that we have a hugely underestimated capacity to create new industries and re-create existing ones. In fact, the half-century-old Standard Industrial Classification (SIC) system published by the U.S. Census was replaced in 1997 by the North America Industry Classification Standard (NAICS) system. The new system expanded the ten SIC industry sectors into twenty sectors to reflect the emerging realities of new industry territories.[5] The services sector under the old system, for example, is now expanded into seven business sectors ranging from information to health care and social assistance.[6] Given that these systems are designed for standardization and continuity, such a replacement shows how significant the expansion of blue oceans has been.

Yet the overriding focus of strategic thinking has been on competition-based red ocean strategies. Part of the explanation for this is that corporate strategy is heavily influenced by its roots in military strategy. The very language of strategy is deeply imbued with military references—chief executive "officers" in "headquarters," "troops" on the "front lines." Described this way, strategy is about confronting an opponent and fighting over a given piece of land that is both limited and constant.[7] Unlike war, however, the history of industry shows us that the market universe has never been constant; rather, blue oceans have continuously been created over time. To focus on the red ocean is therefore to accept the key constraining factors of war—limited terrain and the need to beat an enemy to succeed—and to deny the distinctive strength of the business world: the capacity to create new market space that is uncontested.

The Impact of Creating Blue Oceans

We set out to quantify the impact of creating blue oceans on a company's growth in both revenues and profits in a study of the business launches of 108 companies (see figure 1-1). We found that 86 percent of the launches were line extensions, that is, incremental improvements within the red ocean of existing market space. Yet they accounted for only 62 percent of total revenues and a mere 39 percent of total profits. The remaining 14 percent of the launches were aimed at creating blue oceans. They generated 38 percent of total revenues and 61 percent of total profits. Given that business launches included the total investments made for creating red and blue oceans (regardless of their subsequent revenue and profit consequences, including failures), the performance benefits of creating

FIGURE 1-1

The Profit and Growth Consequences of Creating Blue Oceans

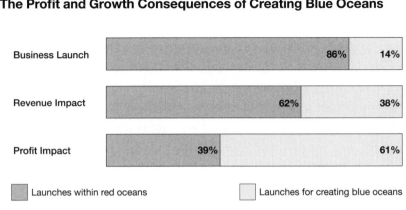

blue waters are evident. Although we don't have data on the hit rate of success of red and blue ocean initiatives, the global performance differences between them are marked.

The Rising Imperative of Creating Blue Oceans

There are several driving forces behind a rising imperative to create blue oceans. Accelerated technological advances have substantially improved industrial productivity and have allowed suppliers to produce an unprecedented array of products and services. The result is that in increasing numbers of industries, supply exceeds demand.[8] The trend toward globalization compounds the situation. As trade barriers between nations and regions are dismantled and as information on products and prices becomes instantly and globally available, niche markets and havens for monopoly continue to disappear.[9] While supply is on the rise as global competition intensifies, there is no clear evidence of an increase in demand worldwide, and statistics even point to declining populations in many developed markets.[10]

The result has been accelerated commoditization of products and services, increasing price wars, and shrinking profit margins. Recent industrywide studies on major American brands confirm this trend.[11] They reveal that for major product and service categories, brands are generally becoming more similar, and as they are becoming more similar people increasingly select based on price.[12] People no longer insist, as in the past, that their laundry detergent be Tide. Nor will they necessarily stick to Colgate when Crest is on sale, and vice versa. In overcrowded industries, differentiating brands becomes harder in both economic upturns and downturns.

All this suggests that the business environment in which most strategy and management approaches of the twentieth century evolved is increasingly disappearing. As red oceans become increasingly bloody, management will need to be more concerned with blue oceans than the current cohort of managers is accustomed to.

From Company and Industry to Strategic Move

How can a company break out of the red ocean of bloody competition? How can it create a blue ocean? Is there a systematic approach to achieve this and thereby sustain high performance?

In search of an answer, our initial step was to define the basic unit of analysis for our research. To understand the roots of high performance, the business literature typically uses the company as the basic unit of analysis. People have marveled at how companies attain strong, profitable growth with a distinguished set of strategic, operational, and organizational characteristics. Our question, however, was this: Are there *lasting* "excellent" or "visionary" companies that continuously outperform the market and repeatedly create blue oceans?

Consider, for example, *In Search of Excellence* and *Built to Last*.[13] The bestselling book *In Search of Excellence* was published twenty years ago. Yet within two years of its publication a number of the companies surveyed began to slip into oblivion: Atari, Chesebrough-Pond's, Data General, Fluor, National Semiconductor. As documented in *Managing on the Edge*, two-thirds of the identified model firms in the book had fallen from their perches as industry leaders within five years of its publication.[14]

The book *Built to Last* continued in the same footsteps. It sought out the "successful habits of visionary companies" that had a long-running track record of superior performance. To avoid the pitfalls of *In Search of Excellence*, however, the survey period of *Built to Last* was expanded to the entire life span of the companies while its analysis was limited to firms more than forty years old. *Built to Last* also became a bestseller.

But again, upon closer examination, deficiencies in some of the visionary companies spotlighted in *Built to Last* have come to light. As illustrated in the recent book *Creative Destruction*, much of the success attributed to some of the model companies in *Built to Last* was the result of industry sector performance rather than the companies themselves.[15] For example, Hewlett-Packard (HP) met the criteria of *Built to Last* by outperforming the market over the long term. In reality, while HP outperformed the market, so did the entire computer-hardware industry. What's more, HP did not even outperform the competition within the industry. Through this and other examples, *Creative Destruction* questioned whether "visionary" companies that continuously outperform the market have ever existed. And we all have seen the stagnating or declining performance of the Japanese companies that were celebrated as "revolutionary" strategists in their heyday of the late 1970s and early 1980s.

If there is no perpetually high-performing company and if the same company can be brilliant at one moment and wrongheaded at another, it appears that the company is not the appropriate unit of analysis in exploring the roots of high performance and blue oceans.

As discussed earlier, history also shows that industries are constantly being created and expanded over time and that industry conditions and boundaries are not given; individual actors can shape them. Companies need not compete head-on in a given industry space; Cirque du Soleil created a new market space in the entertainment sector, generating strong, profitable growth as a result. It appears, then, that neither the company nor the industry is the best unit of analysis in studying the roots of profitable growth.

Consistent with this observation, our study shows that the strategic move, and not the company or the industry, is the right unit of analysis for explaining the creation of blue oceans and sustained high performance. A strategic move is the set of managerial actions and decisions involved in making a major market-creating business offering. Compaq, for example, was acquired by Hewlett-Packard in 2001 and ceased to be an independent company. As a result, many people might judge the company as unsuccessful. This does not, however, invalidate the blue ocean strategic moves that Compaq made in creating the server industry. These strategic moves not only were a part of the company's powerful comeback in the mid-1990s but also unlocked a new multibillion-dollar market space in computing.

Appendix A, "A Sketch of the Historical Pattern of Blue Ocean Creation," provides a snapshot overview of the history of three representative U.S. industries drawn from our database: the auto industry—how we get to work; the computer industry—what we use at work; and the cinema industry—where we go after work for enjoyment. As shown in appendix A, no perpetually excellent company or industry is found. But a striking commonality appears to exist across strategic moves that have created blue oceans and have led to new trajectories of strong, profitable growth.

The strategic moves we discuss—moves that have delivered products and services that opened and captured new market space, with a significant leap in demand—contain great stories of profitable growth as well as thought-provoking tales of missed opportunities by companies stuck in red oceans. We built our study around these strategic moves to understand the pattern by which blue oceans are created and high performance achieved. We studied more than one hundred fifty strategic moves made from 1880 to 2000 in more than thirty industries, and we closely examined the relevant business players in each of these events. Industries ranged from hotels, the cinema, retail, airlines, energy, computers, broadcasting, and construction to automobiles and steel. We analyzed not only winning business players who created blue oceans but also their less successful competitors.

Both within a given strategic move and across strategic moves, we searched for convergence among the group that created blue oceans and within less successful players caught in the red ocean. We also searched for divergence across these two groups. In so doing, we tried to discover the common factors leading to the creation of blue oceans and the key differences separating those winners from the mere survivors and the losers adrift in the red ocean.

Our analysis of more than thirty industries confirms that neither industry nor organizational characteristics explain the distinction between the two groups. In assessing industry, organizational, and strategic variables we found that the creation and capturing of blue oceans were achieved by small and large companies, by young and

old managers, by companies in attractive and unattractive industries, by new entrants and established incumbents, by private and
public companies, by companies in low- and high-tech industries,
and by companies of diverse national origins.

Our analysis failed to find any perpetually excellent company or
industry. What we did find behind the seemingly idiosyncratic success stories, however, was a consistent and common pattern across
strategic moves for creating and capturing blue oceans. Whether it
was Ford in 1908 with the Model T; GM in 1924 with cars styled to
appeal to the emotions; CNN in 1980 with real-time news 24/7; or
Compaq, Starbucks, Southwest Airlines, or Cirque du Soleil—or,
for that matter, any of the other blue ocean moves in our study—the
approach to strategy in creating blue oceans was consistent across
time regardless of industry. Our research also reached out to embrace famous strategic moves in public sector turnarounds. Here
we found a strikingly similar pattern.

Value Innovation: The Cornerstone
of Blue Ocean Strategy

What consistently separated winners from losers in creating blue
oceans was their approach to strategy. The companies caught in
the red ocean followed a conventional approach, racing to beat the
competition by building a defensible position within the existing
industry order.[16] The creators of blue oceans, surprisingly, didn't
use the competition as their benchmark.[17] Instead, they followed a
different strategic logic that we call *value innovation*. Value innovation is the cornerstone of blue ocean strategy. We call it value innovation because instead of focusing on beating the competition,
you focus on making the competition irrelevant by creating a leap
in value for buyers and your company, thereby opening up new and
uncontested market space.

Value innovation places equal emphasis on value and innovation. Value without innovation tends to focus on *value creation* on

an incremental scale, something that improves value but is not sufficient to make you stand out in the marketplace.[18] *Innovation* without value tends to be technology-driven, market pioneering, or
futuristic, often shooting beyond what buyers are ready to accept
and pay for.[19] In this sense, it is important to distinguish between
value innovation as opposed to technology innovation and market
pioneering. Our study shows that what separates winners from losers in creating blue oceans is neither bleeding-edge technology nor
"timing for market entry." Sometimes these exist; more often, however, they do not. Value innovation occurs only when companies
align innovation with utility, price, and cost positions. If they fail
to anchor innovation with value in this way, technology innovators
and market pioneers often lay the eggs that other companies hatch.

Value innovation is a new way of thinking about and executing
strategy that results in the creation of a blue ocean and a break
from the competition. Importantly, value innovation defies one of
the most commonly accepted dogmas of competition-based strategy: the value-cost trade-off.[20] It is conventionally believed that
companies can either create greater value to customers at a higher
cost or create reasonable value at a lower cost. Here strategy is
seen as making a choice between differentiation and low cost.[21] In
contrast, those that seek to create blue oceans pursue differentiation and low cost simultaneously.

Let's return to the example of Cirque du Soleil. Pursuing differentiation and low cost simultaneously lies at the heart of the entertainment experience it created. At the time of its debut, other
circuses focused on benchmarking one another and maximizing
their share of already shrinking demand by tweaking traditional
circus acts. This included trying to secure more famous clowns and
lion tamers, a strategy that raised circuses' cost structure without
substantially altering the circus experience. The result was rising
costs without rising revenues, and a downward spiral of overall circus demand.

These efforts were made irrelevant when Cirque du Soleil appeared. Neither an ordinary circus nor a classic theater production,

Cirque du Soleil paid no heed to what the competition did. Instead of following the conventional logic of outpacing the competition by offering a better solution to the given problem—creating a circus with even greater fun and thrills—it sought to offer people the fun and thrill of the circus *and* the intellectual sophistication and artistic richness of the theater at the same time; hence, it redefined the problem itself.[22] By breaking the market boundaries of theater and circus, Cirque du Soleil gained a new understanding not only of circus customers but also of circus noncustomers: adult theater customers.

This led to a whole new circus concept that broke the value-cost trade-off and created a blue ocean of new market space. Consider the differences. Whereas other circuses focused on offering animal shows, hiring star performers, presenting multiple show arenas in the form of three rings, and pushing aisle concession sales, Cirque du Soleil did away with all these factors. These factors had long been taken for granted in the traditional circus industry, which never questioned their ongoing relevance. However, there was increasing public discomfort with the use of animals. Moreover, animal acts were one of the most expensive elements, including not only the cost of the animals but also their training, medical care, housing, insurance, and transportation.

Similarly, while the circus industry focused on featuring stars, in the mind of the public the so-called stars of the circus were trivial next to movie stars. Again, they were a high-cost component carrying little sway with spectators. Gone, too, are three-ring venues. Not only did this arrangement create angst among spectators as they rapidly switched their gaze from one ring to the other, but it also increased the number of performers needed, with obvious cost implications. And although aisle concession sales appeared to be a good way to generate revenue, in practice the high prices discouraged audiences from making purchases and made them feel they were being taken for a ride.

The lasting allure of the traditional circus came down to only three key factors: the tent, the clowns, and the classic acrobatic acts such as the wheelman and short stunts. So Cirque du Soleil kept the clowns but shifted their humor from slapstick to a more enchanting, sophisticated style. It glamorized the tent, an element that, ironically, many circuses had begun to forfeit in favor of rented venues. Seeing that this unique venue symbolically captured the magic of the circus, Cirque du Soleil designed the classic symbol of the circus with a glorious external finish and a higher level of comfort, making its tents reminiscent of the grand epic circuses. Gone were the sawdust and hard benches. Acrobats and other thrilling acts are retained, but their roles were reduced and made more elegant by the addition of artistic flair and intellectual wonder to the acts.

By looking across the market boundary of theater, Cirque du Soleil also offered new noncircus factors, such as a story line and, with it, intellectual richness, artistic music and dance, and multiple productions. These factors, entirely new creations for the circus industry, are drawn from the alternative live entertainment industry of theater.

Unlike traditional circus shows having a series of unrelated acts, for example, each Cirque du Soleil creation has a theme and story line, somewhat resembling a theater performance. Although the theme is vague (and intentionally so), it brings harmony and an intellectual element to the show—without limiting the potential for acts. Le Cirque also borrows ideas from Broadway shows. For example, it features multiple productions rather than the traditional "one for all" shows. As with Broadway shows, too, each Cirque du Soleil show has an original score and assorted music, which drives the visual performance, lighting, and timing of the acts rather than the other way around. The shows feature abstract and spiritual dance, an idea derived from theater and ballet. By introducing these new factors into its offering, Cirque du Soleil has created more sophisticated shows.

Moreover, by injecting the concept of multiple productions and by giving people a reason to come to the circus more frequently, Cirque du Soleil has dramatically increased demand.

In short, Cirque du Soleil offers the best of both circus and theater, and it has eliminated or reduced everything else. By offering unprecedented utility, Cirque du Soleil has created a blue ocean and has invented a new form of live entertainment, one that is markedly different from both traditional circus and theater. At the same time, by eliminating many of the most costly elements of the circus, it has dramatically reduced its cost structure, achieving both differentiation and low cost. Le Cirque strategically priced its tickets against those of the theater, lifting the price point of the circus industry by several multiples while still pricing its productions to capture the mass of adult customers, who were used to theater prices.

Figure 1-2 depicts the differentiation–low cost dynamics underpinning value innovation.

FIGURE 1-2

Value Innovation: The Cornerstone of Blue Ocean Strategy

Value innovation is created in the region where a company's actions favorably affect both its cost structure and its value proposition to buyers. Cost savings are made by eliminating and reducing the factors an industry competes on. Buyer value is lifted by raising and creating elements the industry has never offered. Over time, costs are reduced further as scale economies kick in due to the high sales volumes that superior value generates.

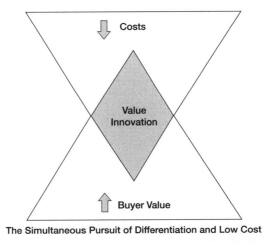

The Simultaneous Pursuit of Differentiation and Low Cost

As shown in figure 1-2, the creation of blue oceans is about driving costs down while simultaneously driving value up for buyers. This is how a leap in value for both the company and its buyers is achieved. Because buyer value comes from the utility and price that the company offers to buyers and because the value to the company is generated from price and its cost structure, value innovation is achieved only when the whole system of the company's utility, price, and cost activities is properly aligned. It is this whole-system approach that makes the creation of blue oceans a sustainable strategy. Blue ocean strategy integrates the range of a firm's functional and operational activities.

In contrast, innovations such as production innovations can be achieved at the subsystem level without impacting the company's overall strategy. An innovation in the production process, for example, may lower a company's cost structure to reinforce its existing cost leadership strategy without changing the utility proposition of its offering. Although innovations of this sort may help to secure and even lift a company's position in the existing market space, such a subsystem approach will rarely create a blue ocean of new market space.

In this sense, value innovation is more than *innovation*. It is about *strategy* that embraces the entire system of a company's activities.[23] Value innovation requires companies to orient the whole system toward achieving a *leap* in value for both buyers *and* themselves. Absent such an integral approach, innovation will remain divided from the core of strategy.[24] Figure 1-3 outlines the key defining features of red and blue ocean strategies.

Competition-based red ocean strategy assumes that an industry's structural conditions are given and that firms are forced to compete within them, an assumption based on what the academics call the *structuralist* view, or *environmental determinism*.[25] In contrast, value innovation is based on the view that market boundaries and industry structure are not given and can be reconstructed by the actions and beliefs of industry players. We call this the

FIGURE 1-3

Red Ocean Versus Blue Ocean Strategy

Red Ocean Strategy	Blue Ocean Strategy
Compete in existing market space.	Create uncontested market space.
Beat the competition.	Make the competition irrelevant.
Exploit existing demand.	Create and capture new demand.
Make the value-cost trade-off.	Break the value-cost trade-off.
Align the whole system of a firm's activities with its strategic choice of differentiation *or* low cost.	Align the whole system of a firm's activities in pursuit of differentiation *and* low cost.

reconstructionist view. In the red ocean, differentiation costs because firms compete with the same best-practice rule. Here, the strategic choices for firms are to pursue either differentiation or low cost. In the reconstructionist world, however, the strategic aim is to create new best-practice rules by breaking the existing value-cost trade-off and thereby creating a blue ocean. (For more discussions on this, see appendix B, "Value Innovation: A Reconstructionist View of Strategy.")

Cirque du Soleil broke the best practice rule of the circus industry, achieving both differentiation and low cost by reconstructing elements across existing industry boundaries. Is Cirque du Soleil, then, really a circus, with all that it eliminated, reduced, raised, and created? Or is it theater? And if it is theater, then what genre— a Broadway show, an opera, a ballet? It is not clear. Cirque du Soleil reconstructed elements across these alternatives, and, in the end, it is simultaneously a little of all of them and none of any of them in their entirety. It created a blue ocean of new, uncontested market space that as of yet has no agreed-on industry name.

Formulating and Executing
Blue Ocean Strategy

Although economic conditions indicate the rising imperative of blue oceans, there is a general belief that the odds of success are lower when companies venture beyond existing industry space.[26] The issue is how to succeed in blue oceans. How can companies systematically maximize the opportunities while simultaneously minimizing the risks of formulating and executing blue ocean strategy? If you lack an understanding of the opportunity-maximizing and risk-minimizing principles driving the creation and capture of blue oceans, the odds will be lengthened against your blue ocean initiative.

Of course, there is no such thing as a riskless strategy.[27] Strategy will always involve both opportunity and risk, be it a red ocean or a blue ocean initiative. But at present the playing field is dramatically unbalanced in favor of tools and analytical frameworks to succeed in red oceans. As long as this remains true, red oceans will continue to dominate companies' strategic agenda even as the business imperative for creating blue oceans takes on new urgency. Perhaps this explains why, despite prior calls for companies to go beyond existing industry space, companies have yet to act seriously on these recommendations.

This book seeks to address this imbalance by laying out a methodology to support our thesis. Here we present the principles and analytical frameworks to succeed in blue oceans.

Chapter 2 introduces the analytical tools and frameworks that are essential for creating and capturing blue oceans. Although supplementary tools are introduced in other chapters as needed, these basic analytics are used throughout the book. Companies can make proactive changes in industry or market fundamentals through the purposeful application of these blue ocean tools and frameworks, which are grounded in the issues of both opportunity and risk. Subsequent chapters introduce the principles that drive the successful formulation and implementation of blue ocean strategy and explain how they, along with the analytics, are applied in action.

There are four guiding principles for the successful formulation of blue ocean strategy. Chapters 3 to 6 address these in turn. Chapter 3 identifies the paths by which you can systematically create uncontested market space across diverse industry domains, hence attenuating *search risk*. It teaches you how to make the competition irrelevant by looking across the six conventional boundaries of competition to open up commercially important blue oceans. The six paths focus on looking across alternative industries, across strategic groups, across buyer groups, across complementary product and service offerings, across the functional-emotional orientation of an industry, and even across time.

Chapter 4 shows how to design a company's strategic planning process to go beyond incremental improvements to create value innovations. It presents an alternative to the existing strategic planning process, which is often criticized as a number-crunching exercise that keeps companies locked into making incremental improvements. This principle tackles *planning risk*. Using a visualizing approach that drives you to focus on the big picture rather than to be submerged in numbers and jargon, this chapter proposes a four-step planning process whereby you can build a strategy that creates and captures blue ocean opportunities.

Chapter 5 shows how to maximize the size of a blue ocean. To create the greatest market of new demand, this chapter challenges the conventional practice of aiming for finer segmentation to better meet existing customer preferences. This practice often results in increasingly small target markets. Instead, this chapter shows you how to aggregate demand, not by focusing on the differences that separate customers but by building on the powerful commonalities across noncustomers to maximize the size of the blue ocean being created and new demand being unlocked, hence minimizing *scale risk*.

Chapter 6 lays out the design of a strategy that allows you not only to provide a leap in value to the mass of buyers but also to build a viable business model to produce and maintain profitable growth for itself. It shows you how to ensure that your company builds a business model that profits from the blue ocean it is creating. It addresses *business model risk*. The chapter articulates the sequence in which you should create a strategy to ensure that both you and your customers win as you create new business terrain. Such a strategy follows the sequence of utility, price, cost, and adoption.

Chapters 7 and 8 turn to the principles that drive effective execution of blue ocean strategy. Specifically, chapter 7 introduces what we call *tipping point leadership*. Tipping point leadership shows managers how to mobilize an organization to overcome the key organizational hurdles that block the implementation of a blue ocean strategy. It deals with *organizational risk*. It lays out how leaders and managers alike can surmount the cognitive, resource, motivational, and political hurdles in spite of limited time and resources in executing blue ocean strategy.

Chapter 8 argues for the integration of execution into strategy making, thus motivating people to act on and execute a blue ocean strategy in a sustained way deep in an organization. This chapter

FIGURE 1-4

The Six Principles of Blue Ocean Strategy

Formulation principles	Risk factor each principle attenuates
Reconstruct market boundaries	↓ Search risk
Focus on the big picture, not the numbers	↓ Planning risk
Reach beyond existing demand	↓ Scale risk
Get the strategic sequence right	↓ Business model risk

Execution principles	Risk factor each principle attenuates
Overcome key organizational hurdles	↓ Organizational risk
Build execution into strategy	↓ Management risk

introduces what we call *fair process*. Because a blue ocean strategy perforce represents a departure from the status quo, this chapter shows how fair process facilitates both strategy making and execution by mobilizing people for the voluntary cooperation needed to execute blue ocean strategy. It deals with *management risk* associated with people's attitudes and behaviors.

Figure 1-4 highlights the six principles driving the successful formulation and execution of blue ocean strategy and the risks that these principles attenuate.

Chapter 9 discusses the dynamic aspects of blue ocean strategy—the issues of sustainability and renewal.

Let's now move on to chapter 2, where we lay out the basic analytical tools and frameworks that will be used throughout this book in the formulation and execution of blue ocean strategy.

CHAPTER 2

Analytical Tools
and Frameworks

W E HAVE SPENT THE PAST DECADE developing a set of analytical tools and frameworks in an attempt to make the formulation and execution of blue ocean strategy as systematic and actionable as competing in the red waters of known market space. These analytics fill a central void in the field of strategy, which has developed an impressive array of tools and frameworks to compete in red oceans, such as the five forces for analyzing existing industry conditions and three generic strategies, but has remained virtually silent on practical tools to excel in blue oceans. Instead, executives have received calls to be brave and entrepreneurial, to learn from failure, and to seek out revolutionaries. Although thought-provoking, these are not substitutes for analytics to navigate successfully in blue waters. In the absence of analytics, executives cannot be expected to act on the call to break out of existing competition. Effective blue ocean strategy should be about risk minimization and not risk taking.

To address this imbalance, we studied companies around the world and developed practical methodologies in the quest of blue oceans. We then applied and tested these tools and frameworks in action by working with companies in their pursuit of blue oceans, enriching and refining them in the process. The tools and frameworks presented here are used throughout this book as we discuss the six principles of formulating and executing blue ocean strategy. As a brief introduction to these tools and frameworks, let's look at one industry—the U.S. wine industry—to see how these tools can be applied in practice in the creation of blue oceans.

The United States has the third largest aggregate consumption of wine worldwide. Yet the $20 billion industry is intensely competitive. California wines dominate the domestic market, capturing two-thirds of all U.S. wine sales. These wines compete head-to-head with imported wines from France, Italy, and Spain and New World wines from countries such as Chile, Australia, and Argentina, which have increasingly targeted the U.S. market. With the supply of wines increasing from Oregon, Washington, and New York state and with newly mature vineyard plantings in California, the number of wines has exploded. Yet the U.S. consumer base has essentially remained stagnant. The United States remains stuck at thirty-first place in world per capita wine consumption.

The intense competition has fueled ongoing industry consolidation. The top eight companies produce more than 75 percent of the wine in the United States, and the estimated one thousand six hundred other wineries produce the remaining 25 percent. The dominance of a few key players allows them to leverage distributors to gain shelf space and put millions of dollars into above-the-line marketing budgets. There is a simultaneous consolidation of retailers and distributors across the United States, something that raises their bargaining power against the plethora of wine makers. Titanic battles are being fought for retail and distribution space. It is no surprise that weak, poorly run companies are increasingly being swept aside. Downward pressure on wine prices has set in.

In short, the U.S. wine industry faces intense competition, mounting price pressure, increasing bargaining power on the part of retail and distribution channels, and flat demand despite overwhelming choice. Following conventional strategic thinking, the industry is hardly attractive. For strategists, the critical question is, How do you break out of this red ocean of bloody competition to make the competition irrelevant? How do you open up and capture a blue ocean of uncontested market space?

To address these questions, we turn to the *strategy canvas*, an analytic framework that is central to value innovation and the creation of blue oceans.

The Strategy Canvas

The strategy canvas is both a diagnostic and an action framework for building a compelling blue ocean strategy. It serves two purposes. First, it captures the current state of play in the known market space. This allows you to understand where the competition is currently investing, the factors the industry currently competes on in products, service, and delivery, and what customers receive from the existing competitive offerings on the market. Figure 2-1 captures all this information in graphic form. The horizontal axis captures the range of factors the industry competes on and invests in.

In the case of the U.S. wine industry, there are seven principal factors:

- Price per bottle of wine

- An elite, refined image in packaging, including labels announcing the wine medals won and the use of esoteric enological terminology to stress the art and science of wine making

- Above-the-line marketing to raise consumer awareness in a crowded market and to encourage distributors and retailers to give prominence to a particular wine house

FIGURE 2-1

The Strategy Canvas of the U.S. Wine Industry in the Late 1990s

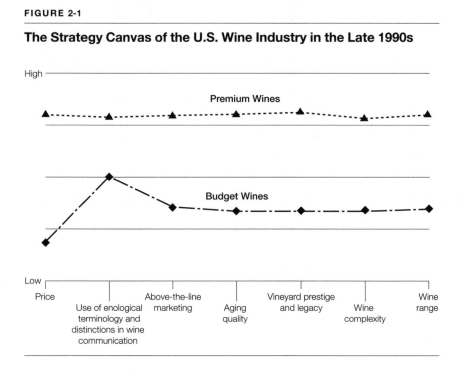

- Aging quality of wine

- The prestige of a wine's vineyard and its legacy (hence the appellations of estates and chateaux and references to the historic age of the establishment)

- The complexity and sophistication of a wine's taste, including such things as tannins and oak

- A diverse range of wines to cover all varieties of grapes and consumer preferences from Chardonnay to Merlot, and so on

These factors are viewed as key to the promotion of wine as a unique beverage for the informed wine drinker, worthy of special occasions.

That is the underlying structure of the U.S. wine industry from the market perspective. Now let's turn to the vertical axis of the

strategy canvas, which captures the offering level that buyers receive across all these key competing factors. A high score means
that a company offers buyers more, and hence invests more, in that
factor. In the case of price, a higher score indicates a higher price.
We can now plot the current offering of wineries across all these
factors to understand wineries' strategic profiles, or value curves.
The *value curve,* the basic component of the strategy canvas, is a
graphic depiction of a company's relative performance across its
industry's factors of competition.

Figure 2-1 shows that, although more than one thousand six
hundred wineries participate in the U.S. wine industry, from the
buyer's point of view there is enormous convergence in their value
curves. Despite the plethora of competitors, when premium brand
wines are plotted on the strategy canvas we discover that from the
market point of view all of them essentially have the same strategic
profile. They offer a high price and present a high level of offering
across all the key competing factors. Their strategic profile follows
a classic differentiation strategy. From the market point of view,
however, they are all different in the same way. On the other hand,
budget wines also have the same essential strategic profile. Their
price is low, as is their offering across all the key competing factors.
These are classic low-cost players. Moreover, the value curves of
premium and low-cost wines share the same basic shape. The two
strategic groups' strategies march in lockstep, but at different alti-
tudes of offering level.

To set a company on a strong, profitable growth trajectory in the
face of these industry conditions, it won't work to benchmark competitors and try to outcompete them by offering a little more for a
little less. Such a strategy may nudge sales up but will hardly drive
a company to open up uncontested market space. Nor is conducting
extensive customer research the path to blue oceans. Our research
found that customers can scarcely imagine how to create uncontested
market space. Their insight also tends toward the familiar "offer me
more for less." And what customers typically want "more" of are those
product and service features that the industry currently offers.

To fundamentally shift the strategy canvas of an industry, you must begin by reorienting your strategic focus from *competitors* to *alternatives*, and from *customers* to *noncustomers* of the industry.[1] To pursue both value and cost, you should resist the old logic of benchmarking competitors in the existing field and choosing between differentiation and cost leadership. As you shift your strategic focus from current competition to alternatives and noncustomers, you gain insight into how to redefine the problem the industry focuses on and thereby reconstruct buyer value elements that reside across industry boundaries. Conventional strategic logic, by contrast, drives you to offer better solutions than your rivals to existing problems defined by your industry.

In the case of the U.S. wine industry, conventional wisdom caused wineries to focus on overdelivering on prestige and the quality of wine at its price point. Overdelivery meant adding complexity to the wine based on taste profiles shared by wine makers and reinforced by the wine show judging system. Wine makers, show judges, and knowledgeable drinkers concur that complexity—layered personality and characteristics that reflect the uniqueness of the soil, season, and wine maker's skill in tannins, oak, and aging processes—equates with quality.

By looking across alternatives, however, Casella Wines, an Australian winery, redefined the problem of the wine industry to a new one: how to make a fun and nontraditional wine that's easy to drink for everyone. Why? In looking at the demand side of the alternatives of beer, spirits, and ready-to-drink cocktails, which captured three times as many U.S. consumer alcohol sales as wine, Casella Wines found that the mass of American adults saw wine as a turnoff. It was intimidating and pretentious, and the complexity of wine's taste created flavor challenges for the average person even though it was the basis on which the industry fought to excel. With this insight, Casella Wines was ready to explore how to redraw the strategic profile of the U.S. wine industry to create a blue ocean. To achieve this, it turned to the second basic analytic underlying blue oceans: the four actions framework.

The Four Actions Framework

To reconstruct buyer value elements in crafting a new value curve, we have developed the *four actions framework*. As shown in figure 2-2, to break the trade-off between differentiation and low cost and to create a new value curve, there are four key questions to challenge an industry's strategic logic and business model:

- Which of the factors that the industry takes for granted should be *eliminated*?

- Which factors should be *reduced well below* the industry's standard?

- Which factors should be *raised well above* the industry's standard?

- Which factors should be *created* that the industry has never offered?

FIGURE 2-2

The Four Actions Framework

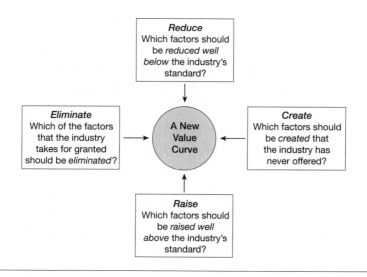

The first question forces you to consider eliminating factors that companies in your industry have long competed on. Often those factors are taken for granted even though they no longer have value or may even detract from value. Sometimes there is a fundamental change in what buyers value, but companies that are focused on benchmarking one another do not act on, or even perceive, the change.

The second question forces you to determine whether products or services have been overdesigned in the race to match and beat the competition. Here, companies overserve customers, increasing their cost structure for no gain.

The third question pushes you to uncover and eliminate the compromises your industry forces customers to make. The fourth question helps you to discover entirely new sources of value for buyers and to create new demand and shift the strategic pricing of the industry.

It is by pursuing the first two questions (of eliminating and reducing) that you gain insight into how to drop your cost structure vis-à-vis competitors. Our research has found that rarely do managers systematically set out to eliminate and reduce their investments in factors that an industry competes on. The result is mounting cost structures and complex business models. The second two factors, by contrast, provide you with insight into how to lift buyer value and create new demand. Collectively, they allow you to systematically explore how you can reconstruct buyer value elements across alternative industries to offer buyers an entirely new experience, while simultaneously keeping your cost structure low. Of particular importance are the actions of eliminating and creating, which push companies to go beyond value maximization exercises with existing factors of competition. Eliminating and creating prompt companies to change the factors themselves, hence making the existing rules of competition irrelevant.

When you apply the four actions framework to the strategy canvas of your industry, you get a revealing new look at old perceived truths. In the case of the U.S. wine industry, by thinking in terms of these four actions vis-à-vis the current industry logic and looking across alternatives and noncustomers, Casella Wines created [yellow tail], a wine whose strategic profile broke from the competition and created a blue ocean. Instead of offering wine as wine, Casella created a social drink accessible to everyone: beer drinkers, cocktail drinkers, and other drinkers of nonwine beverages. In the space of two years, the fun, social drink [yellow tail] emerged as the fastest growing brand in the histories of both the Australian and the U.S. wine industries and the number one imported wine into the United States, surpassing the wines of France and Italy. By August 2003 it was the number one red wine in a 750-ml bottle sold in the United States, outstripping California labels. By mid-2003, [yellow tail]'s moving average annual sales were tracking at 4.5 million cases. In the context of a global wine glut, [yellow tail] has been racing to keep up with sales.

What's more, whereas large wine companies developed strong brands over decades of marketing investment, [yellow tail] leap-frogged tall competitors with no promotional campaign, mass media, or consumer advertising. It didn't simply steal sales from competitors; it grew the market. [yellow tail] brought nonwine drinkers—beer and ready-to-drink cocktail consumers—into the wine market. Moreover, novice table wine drinkers started to drink wine more frequently, jug wine drinkers moved up, and drinkers of more expensive wines moved down to become consumers of [yellow tail].

Figure 2-3 shows the extent to which the application of these four actions led to a break from the competition in the U.S. wine industry. Here we can graphically compare [yellow tail]'s blue ocean strategy with the more than one thousand six hundred wineries competing in the United States. As shown in figure 2-3, [yellow tail]'s value curve stands apart. Casella Wines acted on all four actions—eliminate, reduce, raise, and create—to unlock uncontested market space that changed the face of the U.S. wine industry in a span of two years.

By looking at the alternatives of beer and ready-to-drink cocktails and thinking in terms of noncustomers, Casella Wines created three new factors in the U.S. wine industry—easy drinking, easy to

FIGURE 2-3

The Strategy Canvas of [yellow tail]

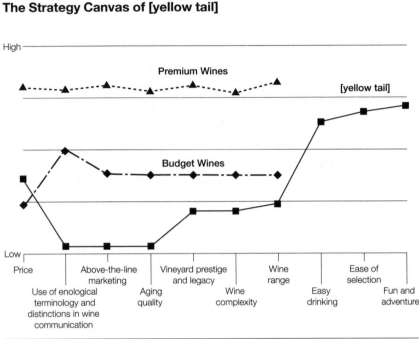

select, and fun and adventure—and eliminated or reduced every-thing else. Casella Wines found that the mass of Americans rejected wine because its complicated taste was difficult to appreciate. Beer and ready-to-drink cocktails, for example, were much sweeter and easier to drink. Accordingly, [yellow tail] was a completely new combination of wine characteristics that produced an uncom-plicated wine structure that was instantly appealing to the mass of alcohol drinkers. The wine was soft in taste and approachable like ready-to-drink cocktails and beer, and had up-front, primary fla-vors and pronounced fruit flavors. The sweet fruitiness of the wine also kept people's palate fresher, allowing them to enjoy another glass of wine without thinking about it. The result was an easy-drinking wine that did not require years to develop an apprecia-tion for.

In line with this simple fruity sweetness, [yellow tail] dramatically reduced or eliminated all the factors the wine industry had long competed on—tannins, oak, complexity, and aging—in crafting fine wine, whether it was for the premium or the budget segment. With the need for aging eliminated, the needed working capital for aging wine at Casella Wines was also reduced, creating a faster payback for the wine produced. The wine industry criticized the sweet fruitiness of [yellow tail] wine, seeing it as significantly lowering the quality of wine and working against proper appreciation of fine grapes and historic wine craftsmanship. These claims may have been true, but customers of all sorts loved the wine.

Wine retailers in the United States offered buyers aisles of wine varieties, but to the general consumer the choice was overwhelming and intimidating. The bottles looked the same, labels were complicated with enological terminology understandable only to the wine connoisseur or hobbyist, and the choice was so extensive that salesclerks at retail shops were at an equal disadvantage in understanding or recommending wine to bewildered potential buyers. Moreover, the rows of wine choice fatigued and demotivated customers, making selection a difficult process that left the average wine purchaser insecure with the choice.

[yellow tail] changed all that by creating ease of selection. It dramatically reduced the range of wines offered, creating only two: Chardonnay, the most popular white in the United States, and a red, Shiraz. It removed all technical jargon from the bottles and created instead a striking, simple, and nontraditional label featuring a kangaroo in bright, vibrant colors of orange and yellow on a black background. The wine boxes [yellow tail] came in were also of the same vibrant colors, with the name [yellow tail] printed boldly on the sides; the boxes served the dual purpose of acting as eye-catching, unintimidating displays for the wine.

[yellow tail] hit a home run in ease of selection when it made retail shop employees the ambassadors of [yellow tail] by giving them Australian outback clothing, including bushman's hats and oilskin jackets to wear at work. The retail employees were inspired by the branded clothing and having a wine they themselves did not feel intimidated by, and recommendations to buy [yellow tail] flew out of their mouths. In short, it was fun to recommend [yellow tail].

The simplicity of offering only two wines at the start—a red and a white—streamlined Casella Wines' business model. Minimizing the stockkeeping units maximized its stock turnover and minimized investment in warehouse inventory. In fact, this reduction of variety was carried over to the bottles inside the cases. [yellow tail] broke industry conventions. Casella Wines was the first company to put both red and white wine in the same-shaped bottle, a practice that created further simplicity in manufacturing and purchasing and resulted in stunningly simple wine displays.

The wine industry worldwide was proud to promote wine as a refined beverage with a long history and tradition. This is reflected in the target market for the United States: educated professionals in the upper income brackets. Hence, the continuous focus on the quality and legacy of the vineyard, the chateau's or estate's historical tradition, and the wine medals won. Indeed the growth strategies of the major players in the U.S. wine industry were targeted at the premium end of the market, with tens of millions invested in brand advertising to strengthen this image. By looking to beer and ready-to-drink cocktail customers, however, [yellow tail] found that this elite image did not resonate with the general public, which found it intimidating. So [yellow tail] broke with tradition and created a personality that embodied the characteristics of the Australian culture: bold, laid back, fun, and adventurous. Approachability was the mantra: "The essence of a great land . . . Australia." There was no traditional winery image. The lowercase spelling of the name [yellow tail], coupled with the vibrant colors and the kangaroo motif, echoed Australia. And indeed no reference to the vineyard was made on the bottle. The wine promised to jump from the glass like an Aussie kangaroo.

The result is that [yellow tail] appealed to a broad cross section of alcohol beverage consumers. By offering this leap in value, [yellow tail] raised the price of its wines above the budget market, pricing them at $6.99 a bottle, more than double the price of a jug wine. From the moment the wine hit the retail shelves in July 2001, sales took off.

The Eliminate-Reduce-Raise-Create Grid

There is a third tool that is key to creation of blue oceans. It is a supplementary analytic to the four actions framework called the *eliminate-reduce-raise-create grid* (see figure 2-4). The grid pushes companies not only to ask all four questions in the four actions framework but also to *act* on all four to create a new value curve. By driving companies to fill in the grid with the actions of eliminating and reducing as well as raising and creating, the grid gives companies four immediate benefits:

- It pushes them to simultaneously pursue differentiation and low costs to break the value-cost trade-off.

FIGURE 2-4

Eliminate-Reduce-Raise-Create Grid: The Case of [yellow tail]

Eliminate	Raise
Enological terminology and distinctions	Price versus budget wines
Aging qualities	Retail store involvement
Above-the-line marketing	
Reduce	**Create**
Wine complexity	Easy drinking
Wine range	Ease of selection
Vineyard prestige	Fun and adventure

- It immediately flags companies that are focused only on raising and creating and thereby lifting their cost structure and
often overengineering products and services—a common
plight in many companies.

- It is easily understood by managers at any level, creating a
high level of engagement in its application.

- Because completing the grid is a challenging task, it drives
companies to robustly scrutinize every factor the industry
competes on, making them discover the range of implicit
assumptions they make unconsciously in competing.

Figure 2-5, the eliminate-reduce-raise-create grid for Cirque du
Soleil, provides another snapshot of this tool in action and shows
what it reveals. Worth noting is the range of factors that an industry has long competed on that companies discover can be eliminated and reduced. In the case of Cirque du Soleil, it eliminated
several factors from traditional circuses, such as animal shows,

FIGURE 2-5

Eliminate-Reduce-Raise-Create Grid: The Case of Cirque du Soleil

Eliminate	Raise
Star performers	Unique venue
Animal shows	
Aisle concession sales	
Multiple show arenas	
Reduce	**Create**
Fun and humor	Theme
Thrill and danger	Refined environment
	Multiple productions
	Artistic music and dance

star performers, and multiple show arenas. These factors had long been taken for granted in the traditional circus industry, which never questioned their ongoing relevance. However, there was increasing public discomfort with the use of animals. Moreover, animal acts are one of the most expensive elements; not only is there the cost of the animals, but also their training, medical care, housing, insurance, and transportation. Similarly, although the circus industry focused on featuring stars, in the mind of the public the so-called stars of the circus were trivial next to movie stars. Again, they were a high-cost component carrying little sway with spectators. Gone, too, are three-ring venues. Not only did these create angst among spectators as they rapidly switched their gaze from one ring to the other, but they also increased the number of performers needed, with the obvious cost implications.

Three Characteristics of a Good Strategy

[yellow tail], like Cirque du Soleil, created a unique and exceptional value curve to unlock a blue ocean. As shown in the strategy canvas, [yellow tail]'s value curve has *focus*; the company does not diffuse its efforts across all key factors of competition. The shape of its value curve *diverges* from the other players', a result of not benchmarking competitors but instead looking across alternatives. The *tagline* of [yellow tail]'s strategic profile is clear: a fun and simple wine to be enjoyed every day.

When expressed through a value curve, then, an effective blue ocean strategy like [yellow tail]'s has three complementary qualities: focus, divergence, and a compelling tagline. Without these qualities, a company's strategy will likely be muddled, undifferentiated, and hard to communicate with a high cost structure. The four actions of creating a new value curve should be well guided toward building a company's strategic profile with these characteristics. These three characteristics serve as an initial litmus test of the commercial viability of blue ocean ideas.

FIGURE 2-6

The Strategy Canvas of Southwest Airlines

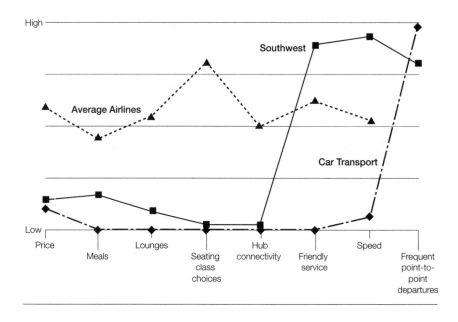

A look at Southwest Airlines' strategic profile illustrates how these three qualities underlie the company's effective strategy in reinventing the short-haul airline industry via value innovation (see figure 2-6). Southwest Airlines created a blue ocean by breaking the trade-offs customers had to make between the speed of airplanes and the economy and flexibility of car transport. To achieve this, Southwest offered high-speed transport with frequent and flexible departures at prices attractive to the mass of buyers. By eliminating and reducing certain factors of competition and raising others in the traditional airline industry, as well as by creating new factors drawn from the alternative industry of car transport, Southwest Airlines was able to offer unprecedented utility for air travelers and achieve a leap in value with a low-cost business model.

The value curve of Southwest Airlines differs distinctively from those of its competitors in the strategy canvas. Its strategic profile is a typical example of a compelling blue ocean strategy.

Focus

Every great strategy has focus, and a company's strategic profile, or value curve, should clearly show it. Looking at Southwest's profile, we can see at once that the company emphasizes only three factors: friendly service, speed, and frequent point-to-point departures. By focusing in this way, Southwest has been able to price against car transportation; it doesn't make extra investments in meals, lounges, and seating choices. By contrast, Southwest's traditional competitors invest in all the airline industry's competitive factors, making it much more difficult for them to match Southwest's prices. Investing across the board, these companies let their competitors' moves set their own agendas. Costly business models result.

Divergence

When a company's strategy is formed reactively as it tries to keep up with the competition, it loses its uniqueness. Consider the similarities in most airlines' meals and business-class lounges. On the strategy canvas, therefore, reactive strategists tend to share the same strategic profile. Indeed, in the case of Southwest, the value curves of the company's competitors are virtually identical and therefore can be summarized on the strategy canvas with a single value curve.

In contrast, the value curves of blue ocean strategists always stand apart. By applying the four actions of eliminating, reducing, raising, and creating, they differentiate their profiles from the industry's average profile. Southwest, for example, pioneered point-to-point travel between midsize cities; previously, the industry operated through hub-and-spoke systems.

Compelling Tagline

A good strategy has a clear-cut and compelling tagline. "The speed of a plane at the price of a car—whenever you need it." That's the tagline of Southwest Airlines, or at least it could be. What could

Southwest's competitors say? Even the most proficient ad agency would have difficulty reducing the conventional offering of lunches, seat choices, lounges, and hub links, with standard service, slower speeds, and higher prices into a memorable tagline. A good tagline must not only deliver a clear message but also advertise an offering truthfully, or else customers will lose trust and interest. In fact, a good way to test the effectiveness and strength of a strategy is to look at whether it contains a strong and authentic tagline.

As shown in figure 2-7, Cirque du Soleil's strategic profile also meets the three criteria that define blue ocean strategy: focus, divergence, and a compelling tagline. Cirque du Soleil's strategy canvas allows us to graphically compare its strategic profile with those of its major competitors. The canvas shows clearly the extent of Cirque du Soleil's departure from the conventional logic of the circus. The figure shows that the value curve of Ringling Bros. and Barnum & Bailey is the same basic shape as those of smaller regional circuses. The main difference is that regional circuses

FIGURE 2-7

The Strategy Canvas of Cirque du Soleil

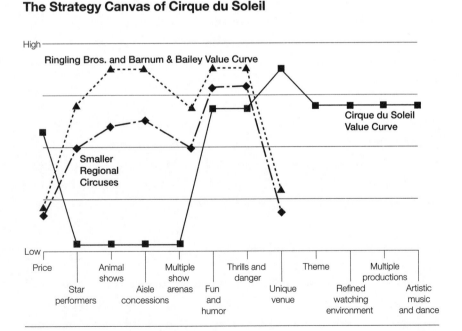

offer less of each competing factor because of their restricted resources.

By contrast, Cirque du Soleil's value curve stands apart. It has new and noncircus factors such as theme, multiple productions, re-fined watching environment, and artistic music and dance. These factors, entirely new creations for the circus industry, are drawn from the alternative live entertainment industry of theater. In this way, the strategy canvas clearly depicts the traditional factors that affect competition among industry players, as well as new factors that lead to creation of new market space and that shift the strategy canvas of an industry.

[yellow tail], Cirque du Soleil, and Southwest Airlines created blue oceans in very different business situations and industrial contexts. However, their strategic profiles shared the same three characteristics: focus, divergence, and a compelling tagline. These three criteria guide companies in carrying out the process of re-construction to arrive at a breakthrough in value both for buyers and for themselves.

Reading the Value Curves

The strategy canvas enables companies to see the future in the present. To achieve this, companies must understand how to read value curves. Embedded in the value curves of an industry is a wealth of strategic knowledge on the current status and future of a business.

A Blue Ocean Strategy

The first question the value curves answer is whether a business de-serves to be a winner. When a company's value curve, or its com-petitors', meets the three criteria that define a good blue ocean strategy—focus, divergence, and a compelling tagline that speaks to the market—the company is on the right track. These three criteria serve as an initial litmus test of the commercial viability of blue ocean ideas.

On the other hand, when a company's value curve lacks focus, its cost structure will tend to be high and its business model complex in implementation and execution. When it lacks divergence, a company's strategy is a me-too, with no reason to stand apart in the marketplace. When it lacks a compelling tagline that speaks to buyers, it is likely to be internally driven or a classic example of innovation for innovation's sake with no great commercial potential and no natural take-off capability.

A Company Caught in the Red Ocean

When a company's value curve converges with its competitors, it signals that a company is likely caught within the red ocean of bloody competition. A company's explicit or implicit strategy tends to be trying to outdo its competition on the basis of cost or quality. This signals slow growth unless, by the grace of luck, the company benefits from being in an industry that is growing on its own accord. This growth is not due to a company's strategy, however, but to luck.

Overdelivery Without Payback

When a company's value curve on the strategy canvas is shown to deliver high levels across all factors, the question is, Does the company's market share and profitability reflect these investments? If not, the strategy canvas signals that the company may be oversupplying its customers, offering too much of those elements that add incremental value to buyers. To value-innovate, the company must decide which factors to eliminate and reduce—and not only those to raise and create—to construct a divergent value curve.

An Incoherent Strategy

When a company's value curve looks like a bowl of spaghetti—a zigzag with no rhyme or reason, where the offering can be described as "low-high-low-low-high-low-high"—it signals that the company doesn't have a coherent strategy. Its strategy is likely based on independent substrategies. These may individually make sense and keep the business running and everyone busy, but collectively they do little to distinguish the company from the best competitor or to provide a clear strategic vision. This is often a reflection of an organization with divisional or functional silos.

Strategic Contradictions

Are there strategic contradictions? These are areas where a company is offering a high level on one competing factor while ignoring others that support that factor. An example is investing heavily in making a company's Web site easy to use but failing to correct the site's slow speed of operation. Strategic inconsistencies can also be found between the level of your offering and your price. For example, a petroleum station company found that it offered "less for more": fewer services than the best competitor at a higher price. No wonder it was losing market share fast.

An Internally Driven Company

In drawing the strategy canvas, how does a company label the industry's competing factors? For example, does it use the word *megahertz* instead of *speed*, or *thermal water temperature* instead of *hot water*? Are the competing factors stated in terms buyers can understand and value, or are they in operational jargon? The kind of language used in the strategy canvas gives insight as to whether a company's strategic vision is built on an "outside-in" perspective, driven by the demand side, or an "inside-out" perspective that is operationally driven. Analyzing the language of the strategy canvas helps a company understand how far it is from creating industry demand.

The tools and frameworks introduced here are essential analytics used throughout this book, and supplementary tools are introduced in other chapters as needed. It is the intersection between these analytic techniques and the six principles of formulating and executing blue oceans that allow companies to break from the competition and unlock uncontested market space.

Now we move on to the first principle, reconstructing market boundaries. In the next chapter we discuss the opportunity-maximizing and risk-minimizing paths to creating blue oceans.

PART TWO

Formulating Blue Ocean Strategy

CHAPTER 3

Reconstruct Market Boundaries

THE FIRST PRINCIPLE of blue ocean strategy is to reconstruct market boundaries to break from the competition and create blue oceans. This principle addresses the search risk many companies struggle with. The challenge is to successfully identify, out of the haystack of possibilities that exist, commercially compelling blue ocean opportunities. This challenge is key because managers cannot afford to be riverboat gamblers betting their strategy on intuition or on a random drawing.

In conducting our research, we sought to discover whether there were systematic patterns for reconstructing market boundaries to create blue oceans. And, if there were, we wanted to know whether these patterns applied across all types of industry sectors—from consumer goods, to industrial products, to finance and services, to telecoms and IT, to pharmaceuticals and B2B—or were they limited to specific industries?

We found clear patterns for creating blue oceans. Specifically, we found six basic approaches to remaking market boundaries. We call this the *six paths framework*. These paths have general applicability across industry sectors, and they lead companies into the corridor of commercially viable blue ocean ideas. None of these paths requires special vision or foresight about the future. All are based on looking at familiar data from a new perspective.

These paths challenge the six fundamental assumptions underlying many companies' strategies. These six assumptions, on which most companies hypnotically build their strategies, keep companies trapped competing in red oceans. Specifically, companies tend to do the following:

- Define their industry similarly and focus on being the best within it

- Look at their industries through the lens of generally accepted strategic groups (such as luxury automobiles, economy cars, and family vehicles), and strive to stand out in the strategic group they play in

- Focus on the same buyer group, be it the purchaser (as in the office equipment industry), the user (as in the clothing industry), or the influencer (as in the pharmaceutical industry)

- Define the scope of the products and services offered by their industry similarly

- Accept their industry's functional or emotional orientation

- Focus on the same point in time—and often on current competitive threats—in formulating strategy

The more that companies share this conventional wisdom about how they compete, the greater the competitive convergence among them.

To break out of red oceans, companies must break out of the accepted boundaries that define how they compete. Instead of looking within these boundaries, managers need to look systematically across them to create blue oceans. They need to look across alternative industries, across strategic groups, across buyer groups, across complementary product and service offerings, across the functional-emotional orientation of an industry, and even across time. This gives companies keen insight into how to reconstruct market realities to open up blue oceans. Let's examine how each of these six paths works.

Path 1: Look Across Alternative Industries

In the broadest sense, a company competes not only with the other firms in its own industry but also with companies in those other industries that produce alternative products or services. Alternatives are broader than substitutes. Products or services that have different forms but offer the same functionality or core utility are often *substitutes* for each other. On the other hand, *alternatives* include products or services that have different functions and forms but the same purpose.

For example, to sort out their personal finances, people can buy and install a financial software package, hire a CPA, or simply use pencil and paper. The software, the CPA, and the pencil are largely substitutes for each other. They have very different forms but serve the same function: helping people manage their financial affairs.

In contrast, products or services can take different forms and perform different functions but serve the same objective. Consider cinemas versus restaurants. Restaurants have few physical features in common with cinemas and serve a distinct function: They provide conversational and gastronomical pleasure. This is a very different experience from the visual entertainment offered by cinemas. Despite the differences in form and function, however, people go to a restaurant for the same objective that they go to the movies: to enjoy a night out. These are not substitutes, but alternatives to choose from.

In making every purchase decision, buyers implicitly weigh alternatives, often unconsciously. Do you need a self-indulgent two hours? What should you do to achieve it? Do you go to movie, have a massage, or enjoy reading a favorite book at a local café? The thought process is intuitive for individual consumers and industrial buyers alike.

For some reason, we often abandon this intuitive thinking when we become sellers. Rarely do sellers think consciously about how their customers make trade-offs across alternative industries. A shift in price, a change in model, even a new ad campaign can elicit a tremendous response from rivals within an industry, but the same actions in an alternative industry usually go unnoticed. Trade journals, trade shows, and consumer rating reports reinforce the vertical walls between one industry and another. Often, however, the space between alternative industries provides opportunities for value innovation.

Consider NetJets, which created the blue ocean of fractional jet ownership. In less than twenty years NetJets has grown larger than many airlines, with more than five hundred aircraft, operating more than two hundred fifty thousand flights to more than one hundred forty countries. Purchased by Berkshire Hathaway in 1998, today NetJets is a multibillion-dollar business, with revenues growing at 30–35 percent per year from 1993 to 2000. NetJets' success has been attributed to its flexibility, shortened travel time, hassle-free travel experience, increased reliability, and strategic pricing. The reality is that NetJets reconstructed market boundaries to create this blue ocean by looking across alternative industries.

The most lucrative mass of customers in the aviation industry are corporate travelers. NetJets looked at the existing alternatives and found that when business travelers want to fly, they have two principal choices. On the one hand, a company's executives can fly business class or first class on a commercial airline. On the other hand, a company can purchase its own aircraft to serve its corporate travel needs. The strategic question is, Why would corporations choose one alternative industry over another? By focusing on the key factors that lead corporations to trade across alternatives and eliminating or reducing everything else, NetJets created its blue ocean strategy.

Consider this: Why do corporations choose to use commercial airlines for their corporate travel? Surely it's not because of the long check-in and security lines, hectic flight transfers, overnight stays, or congested airports. Rather, they choose commercial airlines for only one reason: costs. On the one hand, commercial travel avoids the high up-front, fixed-cost investment of a multimillion-dollar jet aircraft. On the other hand, a company purchases only the number of corporate airline tickets needed per year, lowering variable costs and reducing the possibility of unused aviation travel time that often accompanies the ownership of corporate jets.

So NetJets offers its customers one-sixteenth ownership of an aircraft to be shared with fifteen other customers, each one entitled to fifty hours of flight time per year. Starting at $375,000 (plus pilot, maintenance, and other monthly costs), owners can purchase a share in a $6 million aircraft.[1] Customers get the convenience of a private jet at the price of a commercial airline ticket. Comparing first-class travel with private aircraft, the National Business Aviation Association found that when direct and indirect costs—hotel, meals, travel time, expenses—were factored in, the cost of first-class commercial travel was significantly higher. In a cost-benefit analysis for four passengers on a theoretical trip from Newark to Austin, the real cost of the commercial trip was $19,400, compared with $10,100 in a private jet.[2] As for NetJets, it avoids the enormous fixed costs that commercial airlines attempt to cover by filling larger and larger aircraft. NetJets' smaller airplanes, the use of smaller regional airports, and limited staff keep costs to a minimum.

To understand the rest of the NetJets formula, consider the flip side: Why do people choose corporate jets over commercial travel? Certainly it is not to pay the multimillion-dollar price to purchase planes. Nor is it to set up a dedicated flight department to take care of scheduling and other administrative matters. Nor it is to pay so-called deadhead costs—the costs of flying the aircraft from its home base to where it is needed. Rather, corporations buy private jets to dramatically cut total travel time, to reduce the hassle of congested airports, to allow for point-to-point travel, and to gain the benefit of having more productive and energized executives who can hit the ground running upon arrival. So NetJets built on these distinctive strengths. Whereas 70 percent of commercial flights went to only thirty airports across the United States, Net-Jets offered access to more than five thousand five hundred airports across the country, in convenient locations near business centers. On international flights, your plane pulls directly up to the customs office.

With point-to-point service and the exponential increase in the number of airports to land in, there are no flight transfers; trips that would otherwise require overnight stays can be completed in a single day. The time from your car to takeoff is measured in minutes instead of hours. For example, whereas a flight from Washington, D.C., to Sacramento would take 10.5 hours on a commercial airline, it is only 5.2 hours on a NetJets aircraft; from Palm Springs to Cabo San Lucas takes 6 hours commercial, and only 2.1 hours via NetJets.[3] NetJets offers substantial cost savings in total travel time.

Perhaps most appealing, your jet is always available with only four hours' notice. If a jet is not available, NetJets will charter one for you. Last but not least, NetJets dramatically reduces issues related to security threats and offers clients customized in-flight service, such as having your favorite food and beverages ready for you when you board.

By offering the best of commercial travel and private jets and eliminating and reducing everything else, NetJets opened up a multibillion-dollar blue ocean wherein customers get the convenience and speed of a private jet with a low fixed cost and the low variable cost of commercial airline travel (see figure 3-1). And the competition? According to NetJets, in the past seven years fifty-seven companies have set up fractional jet operations; of those, fifty-seven have gone out of business.

The biggest telecommunications success in Japan since the 1980s also has its roots in path 1. Here we are speaking of NTT DoCoMo's i-mode, which was launched in 1999. The i-mode service changed the way people communicate and access information in Japan. NTT DoCoMo's insight into creating a blue ocean came by thinking about why people trade-across the alternatives of mobile phones and the Internet. With deregulation of the Japanese tele-

FIGURE 3-1

The Strategy Canvas of NetJets

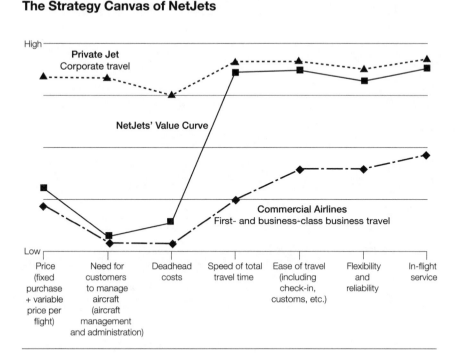

communications industry, new competitors were entering the market and price competition and technological races were the norm. The result was that costs were rising while the average revenue per user fell. NTT DoCoMo broke out of this red ocean of bloody competition by creating a blue ocean of wireless transmission not only of voice but also of text, data, and pictures.

NTT DoCoMo asked, What are the distinctive strengths of the Internet over cell phones, and vice versa? Although the Internet offered endless information and services, the killer apps were e-mail, simple information (such as news, weather forecasts, and a telephone directory), and entertainment (including games, events, and music entertainment). The key downside of the Internet was the far higher price of computer hardware, an overload of information, the nuisance of dialing up to go online, and the fear of giving credit card information electronically. On the other hand, the distinctive strengths of mobile phones were their mobility, voice transmission, and ease of use.

NTT DoCoMo broke the trade-off between these two alternatives, not by creating new technology but by focusing on the decisive advantages that the Internet has over the cell phone and vice versa. The company eliminated or reduced everything else. Its user-friendly interface has one simple button, the i-mode button (*i* standing for interactive, Internet, information, and the English pronoun *I*), which users press to give them immediate access to the few killer apps of the Internet. Instead of barraging you with infinite information as on the Internet, however, the i-mode button acts as a hotel concierge service, connecting only to preselected and preapproved sites for the most popular Internet applications. That makes navigation fast and easy. At the same time, even though the i-mode phone is priced 25 percent higher than a regular cell phone, the price of the i-mode phone is dramatically less than that of a PC, and its mobility is high.

Moreover, beyond adding voice, the i-mode uses a simple billing service whereby all the services used on the Web via the i-mode are billed to the user on the same monthly bill. This dramatically reduces the number of bills users receive and eliminates the need to give credit card details, as on the Internet. And because the i-mode service is automatically turned on whenever the phone is on, users are always connected and have no need to go through the hassle of logging on.

Neither the standard cell phone nor the PC could compete with i-mode's divergent value curve. By the end of 2003 the number of i-mode subscribers had reached 40.1 million, and revenues from the transmission of data, pictures, and text increased from 295 million yen ($2.6 million) in 1999 to 886.3 billion yen ($8 billion) in 2003. The i-mode service did not simply win customers from competitors. It dramatically grew the market, drawing in youth and senior citizens and converting voice-only customers to voice and data transmission customers.

Ironically, European and U.S. counterparts who have been scrambling to unlock a similar blue ocean in the West have so far failed. Why? Our assessment shows that they have been focused on delivering the most sophisticated technology, WAP (wireless application protocol), instead of delivering exceptional value. This has led them to build overcomplicated offerings that miss the key commonalities valued by the mass of people.

Many other well-known success stories have looked across alternatives to create new markets. The Home Depot offers the expertise of professional home contractors at markedly lower prices than hardware stores. By delivering the decisive advantages of both alternative industries—and eliminating or reducing everything else—The Home Depot has transformed enormous latent demand for home improvement into real demand, making ordinary homeowners into do-it-yourselfers. Southwest Airlines concentrated on driving as the alternative to flying, providing the speed of air travel at the price of car travel and creating the blue ocean of short-haul air travel. Similarly, Intuit looked to the pencil as the chief alternative to personal financial software to develop the fun and intuitive Quicken software.

What are the alternative industries to your industry? Why do customers trade across them? By focusing on the key factors that lead buyers to trade across alternative industries and eliminating or reducing everything else, you can create a blue ocean of new market space.

Path 2: Look Across Strategic Groups Within Industries

Just as blue oceans can often be created by looking across alternative industries, so can they be unlocked by looking across *strategic groups*. The term refers to a group of companies within an industry that pursue a similar strategy. In most industries, the fundamental strategic differences among industry players are captured by a small number of strategic groups.

Strategic groups can generally be ranked in a rough hierarchical order built on two dimensions: price and performance. Each jump in price tends to bring a corresponding jump in some dimensions of performance. Most companies focus on improving their competitive position *within* a strategic group. Mercedes, BMW, and Jaguar, for example, focus on outcompeting one another in the luxury car segment as economy car makers focus on excelling over one another in their strategic group. Neither strategic group, however, pays much heed to what the other is doing because from a supply point of view they do not seem to be competing.

The key to creating a blue ocean across existing strategic groups is to break out of this narrow tunnel vision by understanding which factors determine customers' decisions to trade up or down from one group to another.

Consider Curves, the Texas-based women's fitness company. Since franchising began in 1995, Curves has grown like wildfire, acquiring more than two million members in more than six thousand locations, with total revenues exceeding the $1 billion mark. A new Curves opens, on average, every four hours somewhere in the world.

What's more, this growth was triggered almost entirely through word of mouth and buddy referrals. Yet, at its inception, Curves was seen as entering an oversaturated market, gearing its offering to customers who would not want it, and making its offering significantly blander than the competition's. In reality, however, Curves exploded demand in the U.S. fitness industry, unlocking a huge untapped market, a veritable blue ocean of women struggling and failing to keep in shape through sound fitness. Curves built on the decisive advantages of two strategic groups in the U.S. fitness industry—traditional health clubs and home exercise programs—and eliminated or reduced everything else.

At the one extreme, the U.S. fitness industry is awash with traditional health clubs that catered to both men and women, offering a full range of exercise and sporting options, usually in upscale urban locations. Their trendy facilities are designed to attract the high-end health club set. They have the full range of aerobic and strength training machines, a juice bar, instructors, and a full locker room with showers and sauna, because the aim is for customers to spend social as well as exercise time there. Having fought their way across town to health clubs, customers typically spend at least an hour there, and more often two. Membership fees for all this are typically in the range of $100 per month—not cheap, guaranteeing that the market would stay upscale and small. Traditional health club customers represent only 12 percent of the entire population, concentrated overwhelmingly in the larger urban areas. Investment costs for a traditional full-service health club run from $500,000 to more than $1 million, depending on the city center location.

At the other extreme is the strategic group of home exercise programs, such as exercise videos, books, and magazines. These are a small fraction of the cost, are used at home, and generally require little or no exercise equipment. Instruction is minimal, being confined to the star of the exercise video or book and magazine explanations and illustrations.

The question is, What makes women trade either up or down between traditional health clubs and home exercise programs? Most women don't trade up to health clubs for the profusion of special machines, juice bars, locker rooms with sauna, pool, and the chance to meet men. The average female nonathlete does not even want to run into men when she is working out, perhaps revealing lumps in her leotards. She is not inspired to line up behind machines in which she needs to change weights and adjust their incline angles. As for time, it has become an increasingly scarce commodity for the average woman. Few can afford to spend one to two hours at a health club several times a week. For the mass of women, the city center locations also present traffic challenges, something that increases stress and discourages going to the gym.

It turns out that most women trade up to health clubs for one principal reason. When they are at home it's too easy to find an excuse for not working out. It is hard to be disciplined in the confines of one's home if you are not already a committed sports enthusiast. Working out collectively, instead of alone, is more motivating and inspiring. Conversely, women who use home exercise programs do so primarily for the time saving, lower costs, and privacy.

Curves built its blue ocean by drawing on the distinctive strengths of these two strategic groups, eliminating and reducing everything else (see figure 3-2). Curves has eliminated all the aspects of the traditional health club that are of little interest to the broad mass of women. Gone are the profusion of special machines, food, spa, pool, and even locker rooms, which have been replaced by a few curtained-off changing areas.

The experience in a Curves club is entirely different from that in a typical health club. The member enters the exercise room where the machines (typically about ten) are arranged, not in rows facing a television as in the health club, but in a circle to facilitate interchange among members, making the experience fun. The QuickFit circuit training system uses hydraulic exercise machines, which need no adjusting, are safe, simple to use, and nonthreatening. Specifically designed for women, these machines reduce impact stress and build strength and muscle. While exercising, members can talk and support one another, and the social, nonjudgmental atmosphere is totally different from that of a typical health club. There are few if any mirrors on the wall, and there are no men staring at you. Members move around the circle of machines and aerobic pads and in thirty minutes complete the whole workout. The result of reducing and focusing service on the essentials is that prices fall to around $30 per month, opening the market to the broad mass of women. Curves' tagline could be "for the price of a cup of coffee a day you can obtain the gift of health through proper exercise."

Curves offers the distinctive value depicted in figure 3-2 at a lower cost. Compared with the start-up investment of $500,000 to $1 million for traditional health clubs, start-up investments for Curves are in the range of only $25,000 to $30,000 (excluding a $20,000 franchise fee) because of the wide range of factors the company eliminated. Variable costs are also significantly lower, with personnel and maintenance of facilities dramatically reduced and

FIGURE 3-2

The Strategy Canvas of Curves

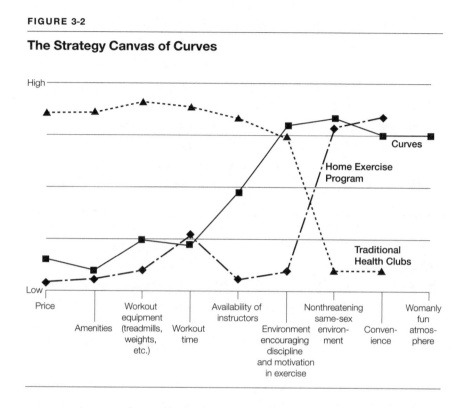

rent reduced because of the much smaller spaces required: 1,500 square feet in nonprime suburban locations versus 35,000 to 100,000 square feet in prime urban locations. Curves' low-cost business model makes its franchises easy to afford and helps explain why they have mushroomed quickly. Most franchises are profitable within a few months, as soon as they recruit on average one hundred members. Established Curves franchises are selling in the range of $100,000 to $150,000 on the secondary market.

The result is that Curves facilities are everywhere in most towns of any size. Curves is not competing directly with other health and exercise concepts; it created new blue ocean demand. As the United States and North America become saturated, management has plans to expand into Europe. Expansion has already begun in Latin America and Spain. By the end of 2004, Curves is expected to reach eight thousand five hundred fitness centers.

Beyond Curves, many companies have created blue oceans by looking across strategic groups. Ralph Lauren created the blue ocean of "high fashion with no fashion." Its designer name, the elegance of its stores, and the luxury of its materials capture what most customers value in haute couture. At the same time, its updated classical look and price capture the best of the classical lines such as Brooks Brothers and Burberry. By combining the most attractive factors of both groups and eliminating or reducing everything else, Polo Ralph Lauren not only captured share from both segments but also drew many new customers into the market.

In the luxury car market, Toyota's Lexus carved out a new blue ocean by offering the quality of the high-end Mercedes, BMW, and Jaguar at a price closer to the lower-end Cadillac and Lincoln. And think of the Sony Walkman. By looking across the high fidelity of boom boxes with the low price and mobility of transistor radios within the audio equipment industry, Sony created the personal portable-stereo market in the late 1970s. The Walkman took share from these two strategic groups. In addition, its leap in value drew new customers, including joggers and commuters, into this blue ocean.

Michigan-based Champion Enterprises identified a similar opportunity by looking across two strategic groups in the housing industry: makers of prefabricated housing and on-site developers. Prefabricated houses are cheap and quick to build, but they are also dismally standardized and have a low-quality image. Houses built by developers on-site offer variety and an image of high quality but are dramatically more expensive and take longer to build.

Champion created a blue ocean by offering the decisive advantages of both strategic groups. Its prefabricated houses are quick to build and benefit from tremendous economies of scale and lower costs, but Champion also allows buyers to choose such high-end finishing touches as fireplaces, skylights, and even vaulted ceilings to give the homes a personal feel. In essence, Champion has changed the definition of prefabricated housing. As a result, far more lower- to middle-income buyers have become interested in purchasing prefabricated housing rather than renting or buying an apartment, and even some affluent people are being drawn into the market.

What are the strategic groups in your industry? Why do customers trade up for the higher group, and why do they trade down for the lower one?

Path 3: Look Across the Chain of Buyers

In most industries, competitors converge around a common definition of who the target buyer is. In reality, though, there is a chain of "buyers" who are directly or indirectly involved in the buying decision. The *purchasers* who pay for the product or service may differ from the actual *users*, and in some cases there are important *influencers* as well. Although these three groups may overlap, they often differ. When they do, they frequently hold different definitions of value. A corporate purchasing agent, for example, may be more concerned with costs than the corporate user, who is likely to be far more concerned with ease of use. Similarly, a retailer may value a manufacturer's just-in-time stock replenishment and innovative financing. But consumer purchasers, although strongly influenced by the channel, do not value these things.

Individual companies in an industry often target different customer segments—for example, large versus small customers. But an industry typically converges on a single buyer group. The pharmaceutical industry, for example, focuses overridingly on influencers: doctors. The office equipment industry focuses heavily on purchasers: corporate purchasing departments. And the clothing industry sells predominantly to users. Sometimes there is a strong economic rationale for this focus. But often it is the result of industry practices that have never been questioned.

Challenging an industry's conventional wisdom about which buyer group to target can lead to the discovery of new blue ocean. By looking across buyer groups, companies can gain new insights into how to redesign their value curves to focus on a previously overlooked set of buyers.

Think of Novo Nordisk, the Danish insulin producer that created a blue ocean in the insulin industry. Insulin is used by diabetics to regulate the level of sugar in their blood. Historically, the insulin industry, like most of the pharmaceutical industry, focused its attention on the key influencers: doctors. The importance of doctors in affecting the insulin purchasing decision of diabetics made doctors the target buyer group of the industry. Accordingly, the industry geared its attention and efforts to produce purer insulin in response to doctors' quest for better medication. The issue was that innovations in purification technology had improved dramatically by the early 1980s. As long as the purity of insulin was the major parameter upon which companies competed, little progress could be made further in that direction. Novo itself had already created the first "human monocomponent" insulin that was a chemically exact copy of human insulin. Competitive convergence among the major players was rapidly occurring.

Novo Nordisk, however, saw that it could break away from the competition and create a blue ocean by shifting the industry's longstanding focus on doctors to the users—patients themselves. In focusing on patients, Novo Nordisk found that insulin, which was supplied to diabetes patients in vials, presented significant challenges in administering. Vials left the patient with the complex and unpleasant task of handling syringes, needles, and insulin, and of administering doses according to his or her needs. Needles and syringes also evoked unpleasant feelings of social stigmatism for patients. And patients did not want to fiddle with syringes and needles outside their homes, a frequent occurrence because many patients must inject insulin several times a day.

This led Novo Nordisk to the blue ocean opportunity of NovoPen, launched in 1985. NovoPen, the first user-friendly insulin delivery solution, was designed to remove the hassle and embarrassment of administering insulin. The NovoPen resembled a fountain pen; it contained an insulin cartridge that allowed the patient to easily carry, in one self-contained unit, roughly a week's worth of insulin. The pen had an integrated click mechanism, making it possible for even blind patients to control the dosing and administer insulin. Patients could take the pen with them and inject insulin with ease and convenience without the embarrassing complexity of syringes and needles.

To dominate the blue ocean it had unlocked, Novo Nordisk followed up by introducing, in 1989, NovoLet, a prefilled disposable insulin injection pen with a dosing system that provided users with even greater convenience and ease of use. And in 1999 it brought out the Innovo, an integrated electronic memory and cartridge-based delivery system. Innovo was designed to manage the delivery of insulin through built-in memory and to display the dose, the last dose, and the elapsed time—information that is critical for reducing risk and eliminating worries about missing a dose.

Novo Nordisk's blue ocean strategy shifted the industry landscape and transformed the company from an insulin producer to a diabetes care company. NovoPen and the later delivery systems swept over the insulin market. Sales of insulin in prefilled devices or pens now account for the dominant share in Europe and Japan, where patients are advised to take frequent injections of insulin every day. Although Novo Nordisk itself has more than a 60 percent share in Europe and 80 percent in Japan, 70 percent of its total turnover comes from diabetes care, an offering that originated largely in the company's thinking in terms of users rather than influencers.

Similarly, consider Bloomberg. In a little more than a decade, Bloomberg became one of the largest and most profitable business-information providers in the world. Until Bloomberg's debut in the early 1980s, Reuters and Telerate dominated the online financial-information industry, providing news and prices in real time to the brokerage and investment community. The industry focused on purchasers—IT managers—who valued standardized systems, which made their lives easier.

This made no sense to Bloomberg. Traders and analysts, not IT managers, make or lose millions of dollars for their employers each day. Profit opportunities come from disparities in information. When markets are active, traders and analysts must make rapid decisions. Every second counts.

So Bloomberg designed a system specifically to offer traders better value, one with easy-to-use terminals and keyboards labeled with familiar financial terms. The systems also have two flat-panel monitors so that traders can see all the information they need at once without having to open and close numerous windows. Because traders must analyze information before they act, Bloomberg added a built-in analytic capability that works with the press of a button. Before, traders and analysts had to download data and use a pencil and calculators to perform important financial calculations. Now users can quickly run "what if" scenarios to compute returns on alternative investments, and they can perform longitudinal analyses of historical data.

By focusing on users, Bloomberg was also able to see the paradox of traders' and analysts' personal lives. They have tremendous income but work such long hours that they have little time to spend it. Realizing that markets have slow times during the day when little trading takes place, Bloomberg decided to add information and purchasing services aimed at enhancing traders' personal lives. Traders can use these services to buy items such as flowers, clothing, and jewelry; make travel arrangements; get information about wines; or search through real estate listings.

By shifting its focus upstream from purchasers to users, Bloomberg created a value curve that was radically different from anything the industry had seen before. The traders and analysts wielded their power within their firms to force IT managers to purchase Bloomberg terminals.

Many industries afford similar opportunities to create blue oceans. By questioning conventional definitions of who can and should be the target buyer, companies can often see fundamentally new ways to unlock value. Consider how Canon copiers created the small desktop copier industry by shifting the target customer of the copier industry from corporate purchasers to users. Or how

SAP shifted the customer focus of the business application software industry from the functional user to the corporate purchaser to create its enormously successful real-time integrated software business.

What is the chain of buyers in your industry? Which buyer group does your industry typically focus on? If you shifted the buyer group of your industry, how could you unlock new value?

Path 4: Look Across Complementary Product and Service Offerings

Few products and services are used in a vacuum. In most cases, other products and services affect their value. But in most industries, rivals converge within the bounds of their industry's product and service offerings. Take movie theaters. The ease and cost of getting a babysitter and parking the car affect the perceived value of going to the movies. Yet these complementary services are beyond the bounds of the movie theater industry as it has been traditionally defined. Few cinema operators worry about how hard or costly it is for people to get babysitters. But they should, because it affects demand for their business. Imagine a movie theater with a babysitting service.

Untapped value is often hidden in complementary products and services. The key is to define the total solution buyers seek when they choose a product or service. A simple way to do so is to think about what happens before, during, and after your product is used. Babysitting and parking the car are needed before people can go to the movies. Operating and application software are used along with computer hardware. In the airline industry, ground transportation is used after the flight but is clearly part of what the customer needs to travel from one place to another.

Consider NABI, a Hungarian bus company. It applied path 4 to the $1 billion U.S. transit bus industry. The major customers in the industry are public transport properties (PTPs), municipally owned transportation companies serving fixed-route public bus transportation in major cities or counties.

Under the accepted rules of competition in the industry, companies competed to offer the lowest purchase price. Designs were outdated, delivery times were late, quality was low, and the price of options was prohibitive given the industry's penny-pinching approach. To NABI, however, none of this made sense. Why were bus companies focused only on the initial purchase price of the bus, when municipalities kept buses in circulation for twelve years on average? When it framed the market in this way, NABI saw insights that had escaped the entire industry.

NABI discovered that the highest-cost element to municipalities was not the price of the bus per se, the factor the whole industry competed on, but rather the costs that came after the bus was purchased: the maintenance of running the bus over its twelve-year life cycle. Repairs after traffic accidents, fuel usage, wear and tear on parts that frequently needed to be replaced due to the bus's heavy weight, preventive body work to stop rusting, and the like—these were the highest-cost factors to municipalities. With new demands for clean air being placed on municipalities, the cost for public transport *not* being environmentally friendly was also beginning to be felt. Yet despite all these costs, which outstripped the initial bus price, the industry had virtually overlooked the complementary activity of maintenance and life-cycle costs.

This made NABI realize that the transit bus industry did not have to be a commodity-price-driven industry but that bus companies, focusing on selling buses at the lowest possible price, had made it that way. By looking at the total solution of complementary activities, NABI created a bus unlike any the industry had seen before. Buses were normally made from steel, which was heavy, corrosive, and hard to repair after accidents because entire panels had to be replaced. NABI adopted fiberglass in making its buses, a practice that killed *five* birds with one stone. Fiberglass bodies substantially cut the costs of preventive maintenance by being corrosion-free. It made body repairs faster, cheaper, and easier because fiberglass does not require panel replacements for dents and accidents; rather, damaged parts are simply cut out and new fiberglass materials are easily soldered. At the same time, its light weight (30–35 percent lighter than steel) cut fuel consumption and emissions substantially, making the buses more environmentally friendly. Moreover, its light weight allowed NABI to use not only lower-powered engines but also fewer axles, resulting in lower manufacturing costs and more space inside the bus.

In this way, NABI created a value curve that is radically divergent from the industry's average curve. As you can see in figure 3-3, by building its buses in lightweight fiberglass, NABI eliminated or significantly reduced costs related to corrosion prevention, maintenance, and fuel consumption. As a result, even though NABI charged a higher initial purchase price than the average price of the industry, it offered its buses at a much lower life-cycle cost to municipalities. With much lighter emissions, the NABI buses

FIGURE 3-3

The Strategy Canvas of the U.S. Municipal Bus Industry, Circa 2001

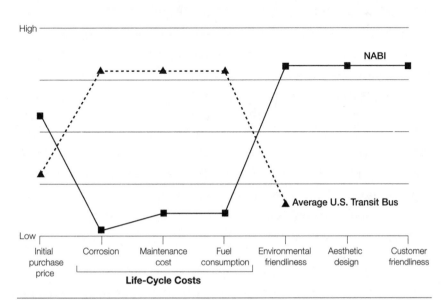

raised the level of environmental friendliness high above the industry standard. Moreover, the higher price NABI charged allowed it to create factors unprecedented in the industry, such as modern aesthetic design and customer friendliness, including lower floors for easy mounting and more seats for less standing. These boosted demand for transit bus service, generating more revenues for municipalities. NABI changed the way municipalities saw their revenues and costs involved in transit bus service. NABI created exceptional value for the buyers—in this case for both municipalities and end users—at a low life-cycle cost.

Not surprisingly, both municipalities and riders loved the new buses. NABI has captured 20 percent of the U.S. market since its inception in 1993, quickly vying for the number one slot in market share, growth, and profitability. NABI, based in Hungary, created a blue ocean that made the competition irrelevant in the United States, creating a win-win for all: itself, municipalities, and citizens. It has accumulated more than $1 billion in orders and was named by the Economist Intelligence Unit in October 2002 as one of the thirty most successful companies in the world.

Similarly, consider the British teakettle industry, which, despite its importance to British culture, had flat sales and shrinking profit margins until Philips Electronics came along with a teakettle that turned the red ocean blue. By thinking in terms of complementary products and services, Philips saw that the biggest issue the British had in brewing tea was not in the kettle itself but in the complementary product of water, which had to be boiled in the kettle. The issue was the lime scale found in tap water. The lime scale accumulated in kettles as the water was boiled, and later found its way into the freshly brewed tea. The phlegmatic British typically took a teaspoon and went fishing to capture the off-putting lime scale before drinking home-brewed tea. To the kettle industry, the water issue was not its problem. It was the problem of another industry—the public water supply.

By thinking in terms of solving the major pain points in customers' total solution, Philips saw the water problem as its opportunity. The result: Philips created a kettle having a mouth filter that effectively captured the lime scale as the water was poured. Lime scale would never again be found swimming in British home-brewed tea. The industry was again kick-started on a strong growth trajectory as people began replacing their old kettles with the new filtered kettles.

There are many other examples of companies that have followed this path to create a blue ocean. Borders and Barnes & Noble (B&N) superstores redefined the scope of the services they offer. They transformed the product they sell from the book itself into the pleasure of reading and intellectual exploration, adding lounges, knowledgeable staff, and coffee bars to create an environment that celebrates reading and learning. In less than six years, Borders and B&N emerged as the two largest bookstore chains in the United States, with more than one thousand seventy superstores between them. Virgin Entertainment's megastores combine CDs, videos, computer games, and stereo and audio equipment to satisfy buyers' complete entertainment needs. Dyson designs its vacuum cleaners to eliminate the cost and annoyance of having to buy and change vacuum cleaner bags. Zeneca's Salick cancer centers combine all the cancer treatments their patients might need under one roof so that they don't have to go from one specialized center to another, making separate appointments for each service they require.

What is the context in which your product or service is used? What happens before, during, and after? Can you identify the pain points? How can you eliminate these pain points through a complementary product or service offering?

Path 5: Look Across Functional or Emotional Appeal to Buyers

Competition in an industry tends to converge not only on an accepted notion of the scope of its products and services but also on one of two possible bases of appeal. Some industries compete principally on price and function largely on calculations of utility; their appeal is rational. Other industries compete largely on feelings; their appeal is emotional.

Yet the appeal of most products or services is rarely intrinsically one or the other. Rather it is usually a result of the way companies have competed in the past, which has unconsciously educated consumers on what to expect. Companies' behavior affects buyers' expectations in a reinforcing cycle. Over time, functionally oriented industries become more functionally oriented; emotionally oriented industries become more emotionally oriented. No wonder market research rarely reveals new insights into what attracts customers. Industries have trained customers in what to expect. When surveyed, they echo back: more of the same for less.

When companies are willing to challenge the functional-emotional orientation of their industry, they often find new market space. We have observed two common patterns. Emotionally oriented industries offer many extras that add price without enhancing functionality. Stripping away those extras may create a fundamentally simpler, lower-priced, lower-cost business model that customers would welcome. Conversely, functionally oriented industries can often infuse commodity products with new life by adding a dose of emotion and, in so doing, can stimulate new demand.

Two well-known examples are Swatch, which transformed the functionally driven budget watch industry into an emotionally driven fashion statement, or The Body Shop, which did the reverse, transforming the emotionally driven industry of cosmetics into a functional, no-nonsense cosmetics house. In addition, consider the experience of QB (Quick Beauty) House. QB House created a blue ocean in the Japanese barbershop industry and is rapidly growing throughout Asia. Started in 1996 in Tokyo, QB House has blossomed from one outlet in 1996 to more than two hundred shops in 2003. The number of visitors surged from 57,000 in 1996 to 3.5 million annually in 2002. The company is expanding in Singapore and Malaysia and is targeting one thousand outlets in Asia by 2013.

At the heart of QB House's blue ocean strategy is a shift in the Asian barbershop industry from an emotional industry to a highly functional one. In Japan the time it takes to get a man's haircut hovers around one hour. Why? A long process of activities is undertaken to make the haircutting experience a ritual. Numerous hot towels are applied, shoulders are rubbed and massaged, customers are served tea and coffee, and the barber follows a ritual in cutting hair, including special hair and skin treatments such as blow drying and shaving. The result is that the actual time spent cutting hair is a fraction of the total time. Moreover, these actions create a long queue for other potential customers. The price of this haircutting process is 3,000 to 5,000 yen ($27 to $45).

QB House changed all that. It recognized that many people, especially working professionals, do not wish to waste an hour on a haircut. So QB House stripped away the emotional service elements of hot towels, shoulder rubs, and tea and coffee. It also dramatically reduced special hair treatments and focused mainly on basic cuts. QB House then went one step further, eliminating the traditional time-consuming wash-and-dry practice by creating the "air wash" system—an overhead hose that is pulled down to "vacuum" every cut-off hair. This new system works much better and faster, without getting the customer's head wet. These changes reduced the haircutting time from one hour to ten minutes. Moreover, outside each shop is a traffic light system that indicates when a haircut slot is available. This removes waiting time uncertainty and eliminates the reservation desk.

In this way, QB House was able to reduce the price of a haircut to 1,000 yen ($9) versus the industry average of 3,000 to 5,000 yen ($27–$45) while raising the hourly revenue earned per barber nearly 50 percent, with lower staff costs and less required retail space per barber. QB House created this "no-nonsense" haircutting service with improved hygiene. It introduced not only a sanitation facility set up for each chair but also a "one-use" policy, where every customer is provided with a new set of towel and comb. To appreciate its blue ocean creation, see figure 3-4.

Cemex, the world's third-largest cement producer, is another company that created a blue ocean by shifting the orientation of its industry—this time in the reverse direction, from functional to

FIGURE 3-4

The Strategy Canvas of QB House

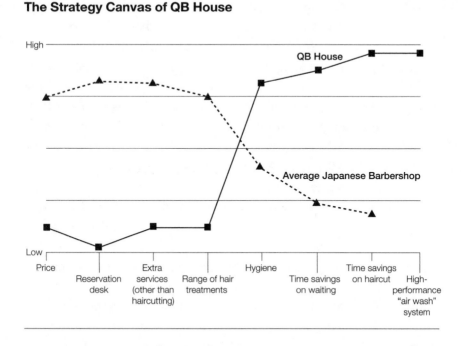

emotional. In Mexico, cement sold in retail bags to the average do-
it-yourselfer represents more than 85 percent of the total cement
market.[4] As it stood, however, the market was unattractive. There
were far more noncustomers than customers. Even though most
poor families owned their own land and cement was sold as a relatively inexpensive functional input material, the Mexican population lived in chronic overcrowding. Few families built additions,
and those that did took on average four to seven years to build only
one additional room. Why? Most of the families' extra money was
spent on village festivals, quinceañeras (girls' fifteen-year birthday
parties), baptisms, and weddings. Contributing to these important
milestone events was a chance to distinguish oneself in the community, whereas not contributing would be a sign of arrogance and
disrespect.

As a result, most of Mexico's poor had insufficient and inconsis-
tent savings to purchase building materials, even though having a

cement house was the stuff of dreams in Mexico. Cemex conservatively estimated that this market could grow to be worth $500 million to $600 million annually if it could unlock this latent demand.[5]

Cemex's answer to this dilemma came in 1998 with its launch of the *Patrimonio Hoy* program, which shifted the orientation of cement from a functional product to the gift of dreams. When people bought cement they were on the path to building rooms of love, where laughter and happiness could be shared—what better gift could there be? At the foundation of Patrimonio Hoy was the traditional Mexican system of *tandas,* a traditional community savings scheme. In a *tanda*, ten individuals (for example) contribute 100 pesos per week for ten weeks. In the first week, lots are drawn to see who "wins" the 1,000 pesos ($93) in each of the ten weeks. All participants win the 1,000 pesos one time only, but when they win, they receive a large amount to make a large purchase.

In traditional *tandas* the "winning" family would spend the windfall on an important festive or religious event such as a baptism or marriage. In the Patrimonio Hoy, however, the *supertanda* is directed toward building room additions with cement. Think of it as a form of wedding registry, except that instead of giving, for example, silverware, Cemex positioned cement as a loving gift.

The *Patrimonio Hoy* building materials club that Cemex set up consisted of a group of roughly seventy people contributing on average 120 pesos each week for seventy weeks. The winner of the *supertanda* each week, however, did not receive the total sum in pesos but rather received the equivalent building materials to complete an entire new room. Cemex complemented the winnings with the delivery of the cement to the winner's home, construction classes on how to effectively build rooms, and a technical adviser who maintained a relationship with the participants during their project.

Whereas Cemex's competitors sold bags of cement, Cemex was selling a dream, with a business model involving innovative financing and construction know-how. Cemex went a step further, throwing small festivities for the town when a room was finished and thereby reinforcing the happiness it brought to people and the *tanda* tradition.

Since the company launched this new emotional orientation of Cemex cement coupled with its funding and technical services, demand for cement has soared. Around 20 percent more families are building additional rooms, and families are planning to build two to three more rooms than originally planned. In a market that competed on price with slow growth, Cemex enjoys 15 percent *monthly* growth, selling its cement at higher prices (roughly 3.5 pesos). Cemex has so far tripled cement consumption by the mass of do-it-yourself homebuilders—from 2,300 pounds consumed every four years, on average, to the same amount being consumed in fifteen months. The predictability of the quantities of cement sold through the *supertandas* also drops Cemex's cost structure via lower inventory costs, smoother production runs, and guaranteed sales that lower costs of capital. Social pressure makes defaults on *supertanda* payments rare. Overall, Cemex created a blue ocean of emotional cement that achieved differentiation at a low cost.

Similarly, with its wildly successful Viagra, Pfizer shifted the focus from medical treatment to lifestyle enhancement. Likewise, consider how Starbucks turned the coffee industry on its head by shifting its focus from commodity coffee sales to the emotional atmosphere in which customers enjoy their coffee.

A burst of blue ocean creation is under way in a number of service industries but in the opposite direction—moving from an emotional to a functional orientation. Relationship businesses, such as insurance, banking, and investing, have relied heavily on the emotional bond between broker and client. They are ripe for change. Direct Line Group, a U.K. insurance company, for example, has done away with traditional brokers. It reasoned that customers would not need the hand-holding and emotional comfort that brokers traditionally provide if the company did a better job of, for example, paying claims rapidly and eliminating complicated paperwork. So instead of using brokers and regional branch offices, Direct Line uses information technology to improve claims handling, and it passes on some of the cost savings to customers in the form of lower insurance premiums. In the United States, The Vanguard Group (in index funds) and Charles Schwab (in brokerage services) are doing the same thing in the investment industry, creating a blue ocean by transforming emotionally oriented businesses based on personal relationships into high-performance, low-cost functional businesses.

Does your industry compete on functionality or emotional appeal? If you compete on emotional appeal, what elements can you strip out to make it functional? If you compete on functionality, what elements can be added to make it emotional?

Path 6: Look Across Time

All industries are subject to external trends that affect their businesses over time. Think of the rapid rise of the Internet or the global movement toward protecting the environment. Looking at these trends with the right perspective can show you how to create blue ocean opportunities.

Most companies adapt incrementally and somewhat passively as events unfold. Whether it's the emergence of new technologies or major regulatory changes, managers tend to focus on projecting the trend itself. That is, they ask in which direction a technology will evolve, how it will be adopted, whether it will become scalable. They pace their own actions to keep up with the development of the trends they're tracking.

But key insights into blue ocean strategy rarely come from projecting the trend itself. Instead they arise from business insights into how the trend will change value to customers and impact the company's business model. By looking across time—from the value a market delivers today to the value it might deliver tomorrow— managers can actively shape their future and lay claim to a new blue ocean. Looking across time is perhaps more difficult than the previous approaches we've discussed, but it can be made subject to the same disciplined approach. We're not talking about predicting the future, something that is inherently impossible. Rather, we're talking about finding insight in trends that are observable today.

Three principles are critical to assessing trends across time. To form the basis of a blue ocean strategy, these trends must be decisive to your business, they must be irreversible, and they must have a clear trajectory. Many trends can be observed at any one time—for example, a discontinuity in technology, the rise of a new lifestyle, or a change in regulatory or social environments. But usually only one or two will have a decisive impact on any particular business. And it may be possible to see a trend or major event without being able to predict its direction.

In 1998, for example, the mounting Asian crisis was an important trend certain to have a big impact on financial services. But it was impossible to predict the direction that trend would take, and therefore it would have been a risky enterprise to envision a blue ocean strategy that might result from it. In contrast, the euro has been evolving along a constant trajectory as it has been replacing Europe's multiple currencies. It is a decisive, irreversible, and clearly developing trend in financial services upon which blue oceans can be created as the European Union continues to enlarge.

Having identified a trend of this nature, you can then look across time and ask yourself what the market would look like if the trend were taken to its logical conclusion. Working back from that vision of a blue ocean strategy, you can identify what must be changed today to unlock a new blue ocean.

For example, Apple observed the flood of illegal music file sharing that began in the late 1990s. Music file sharing programs such as Napster, Kazaa, and LimeWire had created a network of Internet-savvy music lovers freely, yet illegally, sharing music across the globe. By 2003 more than two billion illegal music files were being traded every month. While the recording industry fought to stop the cannibalization of physical CDs, illegal digital music downloading continued to grow.

With the technology out there for anyone to digitally download music free instead of paying $19 for an average CD, the trend toward digital music was clear. This trend was underscored by the fast-growing demand for MP3 players that played mobile digital music, such as Apple's hit iPod. Apple capitalized on this decisive trend with a clear trajectory by launching the iTunes online music store in 2003.

In agreement with five major music companies—BMG, EMI Group, Sony, Universal Music Group, and Warner Brothers Records—iTunes offered legal, easy-to-use, and flexible à la carte song downloads. iTunes allowed buyers to freely browse two hundred thousand songs, listen to thirty-second samples, and download an individual song for 99 cents or an entire album for $9.99. By allowing people to buy individual songs and strategically pricing them far more reasonably, iTunes broke a key customer annoyance factor: the need to purchase an entire CD when they wanted only one or two songs on it.

iTunes also leapt past free downloading services, providing sound quality as well as intuitive navigating, searching, and browsing functions. To illegally download music you must first search for the song, album, or artist. If you are looking for a complete album you must know the names of all the songs and their order. It is rare to find a complete album to download in one location. The sound quality is consistently poor because most people burn CDs at a low bit rate to save space. And most of the tracks available reflect the tastes of sixteen-year-olds, so although theoretically there are billions of tracks available, the scope is limited.

In contrast, Apple's search and browsing functions are considered the best in the business. Moreover, iTunes music editors include a number of added features usually found in the record shops, including iTunes essentials such as Best Hair Bands or Best Love Songs, staff favorites, celebrity play lists, and *Billboard* charts. And the iTunes sound quality is the highest because iTunes encodes songs in a format called AAC, which offers sound quality superior to MP3s, even those burned at a very high data rate.

Customers have been flocking to iTunes, and recording companies and artists are also winning. Under iTunes they receive 65 percent of the purchase price of digitally downloaded songs, at last financially benefiting from the digital downloading craze. In addition, Apple further protected recording companies by devising copyright protection that would not inconvenience users—who had grown accustomed to the freedom of digital music in the post-Napster world—but would satisfy the music industry. The iTunes Music Store allows users to burn songs onto iPods and CDs up to seven times, enough to easily satisfy music lovers but far too few times to make professional piracy an issue.

Today the iTunes Music Store offers more than 700,000 songs and has sold more than 70 million songs in its first year, with users downloading on average 2.5 million per week. Nielsen//NetRatings estimates that the iTunes Music Store now accounts for 70 percent of the legal music download market. Apple's iTunes is unlocking a blue ocean in digital music, with the added advantage of increasing the attractiveness of its already hot iPod player. As other online music stores enter the fray, the challenge for Apple will be to keep its sights on the evolving mass market and not to fall into competitive benchmarking or high-end niche marketing.

Similarly, Cisco Systems created a new market space by thinking across time trends. It started with a decisive and irreversible trend that had a clear trajectory: the growing demand for high-speed data exchange. Cisco looked at the world as it was and concluded that the world was hampered by slow data rates and incompatible computer networks. Demand was exploding as, among other factors, the number of Internet users doubled roughly every one hundred days. So Cisco could clearly see that the problem would inevitably worsen. Cisco's routers, switches, and other networking devices were designed to create breakthrough value for customers, offering fast data exchanges in a seamless networking environment. Thus Cisco's insight is as much about value innovation as it is about technology. Today more than 80 percent of all traffic on the Internet goes through Cisco's products, and its gross margins in this new market space have been in the 60 percent range.

Similarly, a host of other companies are creating blue oceans by applying path 6. Consider how CNN created the first real-time twenty-four-hour global news network based on the rising tide of globalization. Or how HBO's hit show *Sex and the City* acted on the trend of increasingly urban and successful women who struggle to find love and marry later in life.

What trends have a high probability of impacting your industry, are irreversible, and are evolving in a clear trajectory? How will these trends impact your industry? Given this, how can you open up unprecedented customer utility?

Conceiving New Market Space

By thinking across conventional boundaries of competition, you can see how to make convention-altering, strategic moves that reconstruct established market boundaries and create blue oceans. The process of discovering and creating blue oceans is not about predicting or preempting industry trends. Nor is it a trial-and-error process of implementing wild new business ideas that happen to

FIGURE 3-5

From Head-to-Head Competition to Blue Ocean Creation

	Head-to-Head Competition		Blue Ocean Creation
Industry	Focuses on rivals within its industry	⟶	Looks across alternative industries
Strategic group	Focuses on competitive position within strategic group	⟶	Looks across strategic groups within industry
Buyer group	Focuses on better serving the buyer group	⟶	Redefines the industry buyer group
Scope of product or service offering	Focuses on maximizing the value of product and service offerings within the bounds of its industry	⟶	Looks across to complementary product and service offerings
Functional-emotional orientation	Focuses on improving price performance within the functional-emotional orientation of its industry	⟶	Rethinks the functional-emotional orientation of its industry
Time	Focuses on adapting to external trends as they occur	⟶	Participates in shaping external trends over time

come across managers' minds or intuition. Rather, managers are engaged in a structured process of reordering market realities in a fundamentally new way. Through reconstructing existing market elements across industry and market boundaries, they will be able to free themselves from head-to-head competition in the red ocean. Figure 3-5 summarizes the six-path framework.

We are now ready to move on to building your strategy planning process around these six paths. We next look at how you reframe your strategy planning process to focus on the big picture and apply these ideas in formulating your own blue ocean strategy.

CHAPTER 4

Focus on the Big Picture, Not the Numbers

Y OU NOW KNOW THE PATHS to creating blue oceans. The next question is, How do you align your strategic planning process to focus on the big picture and apply these ideas in drawing your company's strategy canvas to arrive at a blue ocean strategy? This is no small challenge. Our research reveals that most companies' strategic planning process keeps them wedded to red oceans. The process tends to drive companies to compete within existing market space.

Think of a typical strategic plan. It starts with a lengthy description of current industry conditions and the competitive situation. Next is a discussion of how to increase market share, capture new segments, or cut costs, followed by an outline of numerous goals and initiatives. A full budget is almost invariably attached, as are lavish graphs and a surfeit of spreadsheets. The process usually culminates in the preparation of a large document culled from a mishmash of data provided by people from various parts of the organization who often have conflicting agendas and poor communication. In this process, managers spend the majority of strategic thinking time filling in boxes and running numbers instead of thinking outside the box and developing a clear picture of how to break from the competition. If you ask companies to present their proposed strategies in no more than a few slides, it is not surprising that few clear or compelling strategies are articulated.

It's no wonder that few strategic plans lead to the creation of blue oceans or are translated into action. Executives are paralyzed by the muddle. Few employees deep down in the company even know what the strategy is. And a closer look reveals that most plans don't contain a strategy at all but rather a smorgasbord of tactics that individually make sense but collectively don't add up to a unified, clear direction that sets a company apart—let alone makes the competition irrelevant. Does this sound like the strategic plans in your company?

This brings us to the second principle of blue ocean strategy: Focus on the big picture, not the numbers. This principle is key to mitigating the planning risk of investing lots of effort and lots of time but delivering only tactical red ocean moves. Here we develop an alternative approach to the existing strategic planning process that is based not on preparing a document but on drawing a strategy canvas.[1] This approach consistently produces strategies that unlock the creativity of a wide range of people within an organization, open companies' eyes to blue oceans, and are easy to understand and communicate for effective execution.

Focusing on the Big Picture

In our research and consulting work, we have found that drawing a strategy canvas not only visualizes a company's current strategic position in its marketplace but also helps it chart its future strategy. By building a company's strategic planning process around a strategy canvas, a company and its managers focus their main attention on the big picture rather than becoming immersed in numbers and jargon and getting caught up in operational details.[2]

As previous chapters reveal, drawing a strategy canvas does three things. First, it shows the strategic profile of an industry by depicting very clearly the factors (and the possible future factors) that affect competition among industry players. Second, it shows the strategic profile of current and potential competitors, identifying which factors they invest in strategically. Finally, it shows the company's strategic profile—or value curve—depicting how it invests in the factors of competition and how it might invest in them in the future. As discussed in chapter 2, the strategic profile with high blue ocean potential has three complementary qualities: focus, divergence, and a compelling tagline. If a company's strategic profile does not clearly reveal those qualities, its strategy will likely be muddled, undifferentiated, and hard to communicate. It is also likely to be costly to execute.

Drawing Your Strategy Canvas

Drawing a strategy canvas is never easy. Even identifying the key factors of competition is far from straightforward. As you will see, the final list is usually very different from the first draft.

Assessing to what extent your company and its competitors offer the various competitive factors is equally challenging. Most managers have a strong impression of how they and their competitors fare along one or two dimensions within their own scope of responsibility, but very few can see the overall dynamics of their industry. The catering manager of an airline, for example, will be highly sensitive to how the airline compares in terms of refreshments. But that focus makes consistent measurement difficult; what seems to be a very big difference to the catering manager may not be important to customers, who look at the complete offering. Some managers will define the competitive factors according to internal benefits. For example, a CIO might prize the company's IT infrastructure for its data-mining capacity, a feature lost on most customers, who are more concerned with speed and ease of use.

FIGURE 4-1

The Four Steps of Visualizing Strategy

1. Visual Awakening	2. Visual Exploration	3. Visual Strategy Fair	4. Visual Communication
• Compare your business with your competitors' by drawing your "as is" strategy canvas. • See where your strategy needs to change.	• Go into the field to explore the six paths to creating blue oceans. • Observe the distinctive advantages of alternative products and services. • See which factors you should eliminate, create, or change.	• Draw your "to be" strategy canvas based on insights from field observations. • Get feedback on alternative strategy canvases from customers, competitors' customers, and noncustomers. • Use feedback to build the best "to be" future strategy.	• Distribute your before-and-after strategic profiles on one page for easy comparison. • Support only those projects and operational moves that allow your company to close the gaps to actualize the new strategy.

Over the past ten years, we have developed a structured process for drawing and discussing a strategy canvas that pushes a company's strategy toward a blue ocean. A 150-year-old financial services group that we'll call European Financial Services (EFS) is one of the companies that adopted this process to develop a strategy that breaks away from the competition. The resulting EFS strategy yielded a 30 percent revenue boost in its initial year. The process, which builds on the six paths of creating blue oceans and involves a lot of visual stimulation in order to unlock people's creativity, has four major steps (see figure 4-1).

Step 1: Visual Awakening

A common mistake is to discuss changes in strategy before resolving differences of opinion about the current state of play. Another problem is that executives are often reluctant to accept the need for change; they may have a vested interest in the status quo, or they may feel that time will eventually vindicate their previous choices.

Indeed, when we ask executives what prompts them to seek out blue oceans and introduce change, they usually say that it takes a highly determined leader or a serious crisis.

Fortunately, we've found that asking executives to draw the value curve of their company's strategy brings home the need for change. It serves as a forceful wake-up call for companies to challenge their existing strategies. That was the experience at EFS, which had been struggling for a long time with an ill-defined and poorly communicated strategy. The company was also deeply divided. The top executives of EFS's regional subsidiaries bitterly resented what they saw as the arrogance of the corporate executives, whose philosophy, they believed, was essentially "nuts in the field, brains in the center." That conflict made it all the more difficult for EFS to come to grips with its strategic problems. Yet before the firm could chart a new strategy, it was essential that it reach a common understanding of its current position.

EFS began the strategy process by bringing together more than twenty senior managers from subsidiaries in Europe, North America, Asia, and Australia and splitting them into two teams. One team was responsible for producing a value curve depicting EFS's current strategic profile in its traditional corporate foreign exchange business relative to its competitors. The other team was charged with the same task for EFS's emerging online foreign exchange business. They were given ninety minutes, because if EFS had a clear strategy, surely it would emerge quickly.

It was a painful experience. Both teams had heated debates about what constituted a competitive factor and what the factors were. Different factors were important, it seemed, in different regions and even for different customer segments. For example, Europeans argued that in its traditional business, EFS had to offer consulting services on risk management, given the perceived risk-averse nature of its customers. Americans, however, dismissed that as largely irrelevant. They stressed the value of speed and ease of use. Many people had pet ideas of which they were the sole champions. One person in the online team argued, for example, that customers

FIGURE 4-2

The Strategy Canvas of Corporate Foreign Exchange, Offline

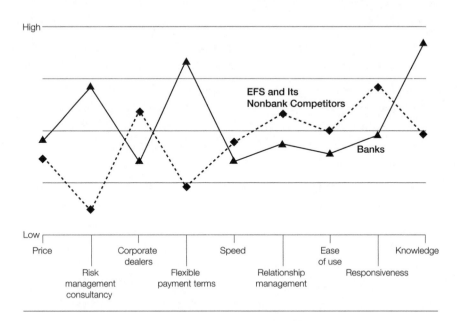

would be drawn in by the promise of instant confirmations of their transactions—a service no one else thought necessary.

Despite these difficulties, the teams completed their assignments and presented their pictures in a general meeting of all participants. Their results are shown in figures 4-2 and 4-3.

The pictures clearly revealed defects in the company's strategy. EFS's traditional and online value curves both demonstrated a serious lack of focus; the company was investing in diverse and numerous factors in both businesses. What's more, EFS's two curves were very similar to those of competitors. Not surprisingly, neither team could come up with a memorable tagline that was true to the team's value curve.

The pictures also highlighted contradictions. The online business, for example, had invested heavily in making the Web site easy to use—it had even won awards for this—but it became apparent

FIGURE 4-3

The Strategy Canvas of Corporate Foreign Exchange, Online

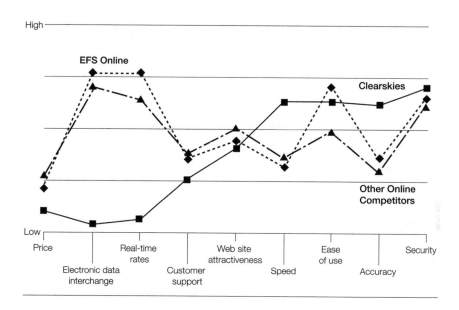

that speed had been overlooked. EFS had one of the slowest Web sites in the business, and that might explain why such a well-regarded site did a relatively poor job of attracting customers and converting them into sales.

The sharpest shocks, perhaps, came from comparing EFS's strategy with its competitors'. The online group realized that its strongest competitor, which we've called Clearskies, had a focused, original, and easily communicable strategy: "One-click E-Z FX." Clearskies, which was growing rapidly, was swimming away from the red ocean.

Faced with direct evidence of the company's shortcomings, EFS's executives could not defend what they had shown to be a weak, unoriginal, and poorly communicated strategy. Trying to draw the strategy canvases had made a stronger case for change than any argument based on numbers and words could have done. This created a strong desire in top management to seriously rethink the company's current strategy.

Step 2: Visual Exploration

Getting the wake-up call is only the first step. The next step is to send a team into the field, putting managers face-to-face with what they must make sense of: how people use or don't use their products or services. This step may seem obvious, but we have found that managers often outsource this part of the strategy-making process. They rely on reports that other people (often at one or two removes from the world they report on) have put together.

A company should never outsource its eyes. There is simply no substitute for seeing for yourself. Great artists don't paint from other people's descriptions or even from photographs; they like to see the subject for themselves. The same is true for great strategists. Michael Bloomberg, before becoming mayor of New York City, was hailed as a business visionary for his realization that the providers of financial information also needed to provide online analytics to help users make sense of the data. But he would be the first to tell you that the idea should have been obvious to anyone who had ever *watched* traders using Reuters or Dow Jones Telerate. Before Bloomberg, traders used paper, pencil, and handheld calculators to write down price quotes and figure fair market values before making buy and sell decisions, a practice that cost them time and money as well as built-in errors.

Great strategic insights like this are less the product of genius than of getting into the field and challenging the boundaries of competition.[3] In the case of Bloomberg, his insight came by switching the focus of the industry from IT purchasers to users: the traders and analysts. This allowed him to see what was invisible to others.[4]

Obviously, the first port of call should be the customers. But you should not stop there. You should also go after noncustomers.[5] And when the customer is not the same as the user, you need to extend your observations to the users, as Bloomberg did. You should not only talk to these people but also watch them in action. Identifying the array of complementary products and services that are consumed alongside your own may give you insight into bundling opportunities. For example, parents who go to the movies will engage a babysitter for the night. As the European cinema operator Kinepolis discovered, adding on-site childcare services helped fill European cinemas. Finally, you need to look at how customers might find alternative ways of fulfilling the need that your product or service satisfies. For example, driving is an alternative to flying, so you should also examine its distinct advantages and characteristics.

EFS sent its managers into the field for four weeks to explore the six paths to creating blue oceans.[6] In this process, each was to interview and observe ten people involved in corporate foreign exchange, including lost customers, new customers, and the customers of EFS's competitors and alternatives. The managers also reached outside the industry's traditional boundaries to companies that did not yet use corporate foreign exchange services but that might in the future, such as Internet-based companies with a global reach like Amazon.com. They interviewed the end users of corporate foreign exchange services—the accounting and treasury departments of companies. And finally, they looked at ancillary products and services that their customers used—in particular, treasury management and pricing simulations.

The field research overturned many of the conclusions managers had reached in the first step of the strategy creation process. For example, account relationship managers, whom nearly everyone had agreed were a key to success and on whom EFS prided itself, turned out to be the company's Achilles' heel. Customers hated wasting time dealing with relationship managers. To buyers, relationship managers were seen as relationship savers because EFS failed to deliver on its promises.

To everyone's astonishment, the factor customers valued most was getting speedy confirmation of transactions, which only one manager had previously suggested was important. The EFS managers saw that their customers' accounting department personnel spent a lot of time making phone calls to confirm that payments had been made and to check when they would be received. Customers received numerous calls on the same subject, and the time wasted in handling them was compounded by the necessity of making further calls to the foreign exchange provider, namely EFS or a competitor.

EFS's teams were then sent back to the drawing board. This time, though, they had to propose a new strategy. Each team had to draw six new value curves using the six path framework explained in chapter 3. Each new value curve had to depict a strategy that would make the company stand out in its market. By demanding six pictures from each team, we hoped to push managers to create innovative proposals and break the boundaries of their conventional thinking.

For each visual strategy, the teams also had to write a compelling tagline that captured the essence of the strategy and spoke directly to buyers. Suggestions included "Leave It to Us," "Make Me Smarter," and "Transactions in Trust." A strong sense of competition developed between the two teams, making the process fun, imbuing it with energy, and driving the teams to develop blue ocean strategies.

Step 3: Visual Strategy Fair

After two weeks of drawing and redrawing, the teams presented their strategy canvases at what we call a *visual strategy fair*. Attendees included senior corporate executives but consisted mainly of representatives of EFS's external constituencies—the kinds of people the managers had met with during their field trips, including noncustomers, customers of competitors, and some of the most demanding EFS customers. In two hours, the teams presented all twelve curves—six by the online group, and six by the offline group. They were given no more than ten minutes to present each curve, on the theory that any idea that takes more than ten minutes to communicate is probably too complicated to be any good. The pictures were hung on the walls so that the audience could easily see them.

After the twelve strategies were presented, each judge—an invited attendee—was given five sticky notes and told to put them next to his or her favorites. The judges could put all five on a single strategy if they found it that compelling. The transparency and immediacy of this approach freed it from the politics that sometimes seem endemic to the strategic planning process. Managers had to rely on the originality and clarity of their curves and their pitches. One began, for example, with the line, "We've got a strategy so cunning that you won't be our customers, you'll be our fans."

After the notes were posted, the judges were asked to explain their picks, adding another level of feedback to the strategy-making process. Judges were also asked to explain why they did not vote for the other value curves.

As the teams synthesized the judges' common likes and dislikes, they realized that fully one-third of what they had thought were key competitive factors were, in fact, marginal to customers. Another one-third either were not well articulated or had been overlooked in the visual awakening phase. It was clear that the executives needed to reassess some long-held assumptions, such as EFS's separation of its online and traditional businesses.

They also learned that buyers from all markets had a basic set of needs and expected similar services. If you met those common needs, customers would happily forgo everything else. Regional differences became significant only when there was a problem with the basics. This was news to many people who had claimed that their regions were unique.

Following the strategy fair, the teams were finally able to complete their mission. They were able to draw a value curve that was a truer likeness of the existing strategic profile than anything they had produced earlier, in part because the new picture ignored the specious distinction that EFS had made between its online and offline businesses. More important, the managers were now in a position to draw a future strategy that would be distinctive as well as speak to a true but hidden need in the marketplace. Figure 4-4 highlights the stark differences between the company's current and future strategies.

As the figure shows, EFS's future strategy eliminated relationship management and reduced investment in account executives,

FIGURE 4-4

EFS: Before and After

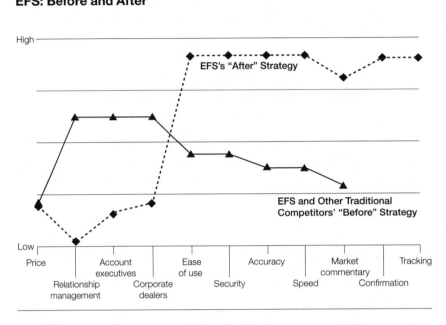

who, from this point on, were assigned only to "AAA" accounts. These moves dramatically reduced EFS's costs because relationship managers and account executives were the highest-cost element of its business. EFS's future strategy emphasized ease of use, security, accuracy, and speed. These factors would be delivered through computerization, which would allow customers to input data directly instead of having to send a fax to EFS.

This action would also free up corporate dealers' time, a large portion of which had been spent completing paperwork and correcting errors. Dealers would now be able to provide richer market commentary, a key success factor. Using the Internet, EFS would send automatic confirmations to all customers. And it would offer a payment-tracking service, just as FedEx and UPS do for parcels. The foreign exchange industry had never offered these services before. Figure 4-5 summarizes EFS's four actions to create value innovation, the cornerstone of blue ocean strategy.

FIGURE 4-5

Eliminate-Reduce-Raise-Create Grid: The Case of EFS

Eliminate	Raise
Relationship management	Ease of use
	Security
	Accuracy
	Speed
	Market commentary
Reduce	**Create**
Account executives	Confirmation
Corporate dealers	Tracking

The new value curve exhibited the criteria of a successful strategy. It displayed more focus than the previous strategy; investments that were made were given a much stronger commitment than before. It also stood apart from the industry's existing me-too curves and lent itself to a compelling tagline: "The FedEx of corporate foreign exchange: easy, reliable, fast, and trackable." By collapsing its online and traditional businesses into one compelling offering, EFS substantially cut the operational complexity of its business model, making systematic execution far easier.

Step 4: Visual Communication

After the future strategy is set, the last step is to communicate it in a way that can be easily understood by any employee. EFS distributed the one-page picture showing its new and old strategic profiles so that every employee could see where the company stood and where it had to focus its efforts to create a compelling future. The senior managers who participated in developing the strategy held meetings with their direct reports to walk them through the picture, explaining what needed to be eliminated, reduced, raised, and created to pursue a blue ocean. Those people passed the message on to their direct reports. Employees were so motivated by the clear game plan that many pinned up a version of the picture in their cubicles as a reminder of EFS's new priorities and the gaps that needed to be closed.

The new picture became a reference point for all investment decisions. Only those ideas that would help EFS move from the old to the new value curve were given the go-ahead. When, for example, regional offices requested that the IT department add links on the Web site—something that in the past would have been agreed to without debate—IT asked them to explain how the new links helped move EFS toward its new profile. If the regional offices couldn't provide an explanation, the request was denied, thereby promoting clarity and not confusion on the Web site. Similarly, when the IT department pitched a multimillion-dollar back-office system to top management, the system's ability to meet the new value curve's strategic needs was the chief metric by which it was judged.

Visualizing Strategy at the Corporate Level

Visualizing strategy can also greatly inform the dialogue among individual business units and the corporate center in transforming a company from a red ocean to a blue ocean player. When business units present their strategy canvases to one another, they deepen their understanding of the other businesses in the corporate portfolio. Moreover, the process also fosters the transfer of strategic best practices across units.

Using the Strategy Canvas

To see how this works, consider how Samsung Electronics of Korea used strategy canvases at its 2000 corporate conference, which was attended by more than seventy top managers, including the CEO. Unit heads presented their canvases and implementation plans to senior executives and to one another. Discussions were heated, and a number of unit heads argued that the freedom of their units to form future strategies was constrained by the degree of competition they faced. Poor performers felt that they had little choice but to match their competitors' offerings. That hypothesis proved to be false when one of the fastest-growing units—the mobile phone business—presented its strategy canvas. Not only did the unit have a distinctive value curve, but it also faced the most intense competition.

Samsung Electronics has institutionalized the use of the strategy canvas in its key business creation decisions by establishing the Value Innovation Program (VIP) Center in 1998. Core cross-functional team members of its various business units come together in the VIP Center to discuss their strategic projects. These discussions typically focus on strategy canvases.

With the value innovation knowledge it has developed, the center, equipped with twenty project rooms, assists the units in making their product and service offering decisions. In 2003, the center completed more than eighty strategic projects and opened more than ten VIP branches to meet business units' rising demands. For example, the world's leading forty-inch LCD TV, launched in December 2002, is the result of one project team's devoted four-month efforts made at the center. So is the world's bestselling mobile phone, the SGH T-100, which has sold more than ten million units.

Since 1999, Samsung Electronics has established an annual Value Innovation corporate conference presided over by all of its top executives. At this conference, Samsung's hit Value Innovation projects are shared through presentations and exhibitions, and awards are given to the best cases. This is one way that Samsung Electronics establishes a common language system, instilling a corporate culture and strategic norms that drive its corporate business portfolio from red to blue oceans.[7]

Do your business unit heads lack an understanding of the other businesses in your corporate portfolio? Are your strategic best practices poorly communicated across your business units? Are your low-performing units quick to blame their competitive situations for their results? If the answer to any of these questions is yes, try drawing, and then sharing, the strategy canvases of your business units.

Using the Pioneer-Migrator-Settler (PMS) Map

Visualizing strategy can also help managers responsible for corporate strategy predict and plan the company's future growth and profit. All the companies that created blue oceans in our study have been pioneers in their industries, not necessarily in developing new technologies but in pushing the value they offer customers to new frontiers. Extending the pioneer metaphor can provide a useful way of talking about the growth potential of current and future businesses.

A company's *pioneers* are the businesses that offer unprecedented value. These are your blue ocean strategists, and they are the most powerful sources of profitable growth. These businesses have a mass following of customers. Their value curve diverges from the competition on the strategy canvas. At the other extreme are *settlers*—businesses whose value curves conform to the basic shape of the industry's. These are me-too businesses. Settlers will not generally contribute much to a company's future growth. They are stuck within the red ocean.

The potential of *migrators* lies somewhere in between. Such businesses extend the industry's curve by giving customers more for less, but they don't alter its basic shape. These businesses offer improved value, but not innovative value. These are businesses whose strategies fall on the margin between red oceans and blue oceans.

A useful exercise for a corporate management team pursuing profitable growth is to plot the company's current and planned portfolios on a *pioneer-migrator-settler* (PMS) map. For the purpose of the exercise, settlers are defined as me-too businesses, migrators are business offerings better than most in the marketplace, and pioneers are the only ones with a mass following of customers.

If both the current portfolio and the planned offerings consist mainly of settlers, the company has a low growth trajectory, is largely confined to red oceans, and needs to push for value innovation. Although the company might be profitable today as its settlers are still making money, it may well have fallen into the trap of competitive benchmarking, imitation, and intense price competition.

If current and planned offerings consist of a lot of migrators, reasonable growth can be expected. But the company is not exploiting its potential for growth, and it risks being marginalized by a company that value-innovates. In our experience the more an industry is populated by settlers, the greater is the opportunity to value-innovate and create a blue ocean of new market space.

This exercise is especially valuable for managers who want to see beyond today's performance. Revenue, profitability, market share, and customer satisfaction are all measures of a company's current position. Contrary to what conventional strategic thinking suggests, those measures cannot point the way to the future; changes in the environment are too rapid. Today's market share is a reflection of how well a business has performed historically. Think of the strategic reversal and market share upset that occurred when CNN entered the U.S. news market. ABC, CBS, and NBC—all with historically strong market shares—were devastated.

Chief executives should instead use value and innovation as the important parameters for managing their portfolio of businesses. They should use innovation because, without it, companies are stuck in the trap of competitive improvements. They should use value because innovative ideas will be profitable only if they are linked to what buyers are willing to pay for.

Clearly, what senior executives should be doing is getting their organizations to shift the balance of their future portfolio toward pioneers. That is the path to profitable growth. The PMS map shown in figure 4-6 depicts this trajectory, showing the scatter plot of a company's portfolio of businesses, where the gravity of

FIGURE 4-6

Testing the Growth Potential of a Portfolio of Businesses

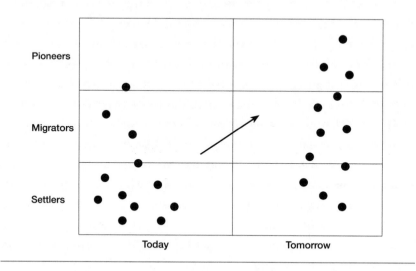

its current portfolio of twelve businesses, expressed as twelve dots, shifts from a preponderance of settlers to a stronger balance of migrators and pioneers.

In pushing their businesses toward pioneers, however, senior executives should be well aware that even though settlers have marginal growth potential, they are frequently today's cash generators. On the other hand, pioneers have maximum growth potential but often consume cash at the outset as they grow and expand. Evidently, senior managers' goal here should be to manage their portfolio of businesses to wisely balance between profitable growth and cash flow at a given point in time.

Overcoming the Limitations
of Strategic Planning

Managers often express discontent, either explicitly or implicitly, with existing strategic planning—the core activity of strategy. To them, strategic planning should be more about collective wisdom building than top-down or bottom-up planning. They think that it should be more conversational than solely documentation-driven, and it should be more about building the big picture than about number-crunching exercises. It should have a creative component instead of being strictly analysis-driven, and it should be more motivational, invoking willing commitment, than bargaining-driven, producing negotiated commitment. Despite this appetite for change, however, scant work exists on building a viable alternative to existing strategic planning, which is the most essential management task in the sense that almost every company in the world not only does it but often takes several grueling months each year to complete the exercise.

Building the process around a picture addresses many of managers' discontents with existing strategic planning and yields much better results. As Aristotle pointed out, "The soul never thinks without an image."

Drawing a strategy canvas and a PMS map is not, of course, the only part of the strategic planning process. At some stage, numbers and documents must be compiled and discussed. But we believe that the details will fall into place more easily if managers start with the big picture of how to break away from the competition. The methods of visualizing strategy proposed here will put strategy back into strategic planning, and they will greatly improve your chances of creating a blue ocean.

How do you maximize the size of the blue ocean you are creating? The following chapter addresses that precise question.

CHAPTER 5

Reach Beyond Existing Demand

N O COMPANY WANTS to venture beyond red oceans only to find itself in a puddle. The question is, How do you maximize the size of the blue ocean you are creating? This brings us to the third principle of blue ocean strategy: Reach beyond existing demand. This is a key component of achieving value innovation. By aggregating the greatest demand for a new offering, this approach attenuates the scale risk associated with creating a new market.

To achieve this, companies should challenge two conventional strategy practices. One is the focus on existing customers. The other is the drive for finer segmentation to accommodate buyer differences. Typically, to grow their share of a market, companies strive to retain and expand existing customers. This often leads to finer segmentation and greater tailoring of offerings to better meet customer preferences. The more intense the competition is, the greater, on average, is the resulting customization of offerings. As companies compete to embrace customer preferences through finer segmentation, they often risk creating too-small target markets.

To maximize the size of their blue oceans, companies need to take a reverse course. Instead of concentrating on customers, they need to look to noncustomers. And instead of focusing on customer differences, they need to build on powerful commonalities in what buyers value. That allows companies to reach beyond existing demand to unlock a new mass of customers that did not exist before.

Think of Callaway Golf. It aggregated new demand for its offering by looking to noncustomers. While the U.S. golf industry fought to win a greater share of existing customers, Callaway created a blue ocean of new demand by asking why sports enthusiasts and people in the country club set had *not* taken up golf as a sport. By looking to why people shied away from golf, it found one key commonality uniting the mass of noncustomers: Hitting the golf ball was perceived as too difficult. The small size of the golf club head demanded enormous hand-eye coordination, took time to master, and required concentration. As a result, fun was sapped for novices, and it took too long to get good at the sport.

This understanding gave Callaway insight into how to aggregate new demand for its offering. The answer was Big Bertha, a golf club with a large head that made it far easier to hit the golf ball. Big Bertha not only converted noncustomers of the industry into customers, but it also pleased existing golf customers, making it a runaway bestseller across the board. With the exception of pros, it turned out that the mass of existing customers also had been frustrated with the difficulty of advancing their game by mastering the skills needed to hit the ball consistently. The club's large head also lessened this difficulty.

Interestingly, however, existing customers, unlike noncustomers, had implicitly accepted the difficulty of the game. Although the mass of existing customers didn't like it, they had taken for granted that that was the way the game was played. Instead of registering their dissatisfaction with golf club makers, they themselves accepted the responsibility to improve. By looking to noncustomers and focusing on their key commonalities—not differences—Callaway saw how to aggregate new demand and offer the mass of customers and noncustomers a leap in value.

Where is your locus of attention—on capturing a greater share of existing customers, or on converting noncustomers of the industry into new demand? Do you seek out key commonalities in what buyers value, or do you strive to embrace customer differences through finer customization and segmentation? To reach beyond existing demand, think noncustomers before customers; commonalities before differences; and desegmentation before pursuing finer segmentation.

The Three Tiers of Noncustomers

Although the universe of noncustomers typically offers big blue ocean opportunities, few companies have keen insight into who noncustomers are and how to unlock them. To convert this huge latent demand into real demand in the form of thriving new customers, companies need to deepen their understanding of the universe of noncustomers.

There are three tiers of noncustomers that can be transformed into customers. They differ in their relative distance from your market. As depicted in figure 5-1, the first tier of noncustomers is closest to your market. They sit on the edge of the market. They are buyers who minimally purchase an industry's offering out of necessity but are mentally noncustomers of the industry. They are waiting to jump ship and leave the industry as soon as the opportunity presents itself. However, if offered a leap in value, not only would they stay, but also their frequency of purchases would multiply, unlocking enormous latent demand.

The second tier of noncustomers is people who refuse to use your industry's offerings. These are buyers who have seen your industry's offerings as an option to fulfill their needs but have voted against them. In the Callaway case, for example, these were sports

FIGURE 5-1

The Three Tiers of Noncustomers

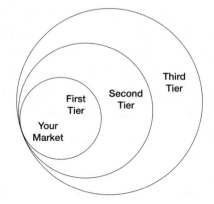

First Tier: "Soon-to-be" noncustomers who are on the edge of your market, waiting to jump ship.
Second Tier: "Refusing" noncustomers who consciously choose against your market.
Third Tier: "Unexplored" noncustomers who are in markets distant from yours.

enthusiasts, especially the country club tennis set, who could have chosen golf but had consciously chosen against it.

The third tier of noncustomers is farthest from your market. They are noncustomers who have never thought of your market's offerings as an option. By focusing on key commonalities across these noncustomers and existing customers, companies can understand how to pull them into their new market.

Let's look at each of the three tiers of noncustomers to understand how you can attract them and expand your blue ocean.

First-Tier Noncustomers

These *soon-to-be* noncustomers are those who minimally use the current market offerings to get by as they search for something better. Upon finding any better alternative, they will eagerly jump ship. In this sense, they sit on the edge of the market. A market becomes stagnant and develops a growth problem as the number of soon-to-be noncustomers increases. Yet locked within these first-tier noncustomers is an ocean of untapped demand waiting to be released.

Consider how Pret A Manger, a British fast-food chain that opened in 1988, has expanded its blue ocean by tapping into the huge latent demand of first-tier noncustomers. Before Pret, professionals in European city centers principally frequented restaurants for lunch. Sit-down restaurants offered a nice meal and setting. However, the number of first-tier noncustomers was high and rising. Growing concerns over the need for healthy eating gave people second thoughts about eating out in restaurants. And professionals did not always have time for a sit-down meal. Some restaurants were also too expensive for lunch on a daily basis. So professionals were increasingly grabbing something on the run, bringing a brown bag from home, or even skipping lunch.

These first-tier noncustomers were in search of better solutions. Although there were numerous differences across them, they shared three key commonalities: They wanted lunch fast, they wanted it fresh and healthy, and they wanted it at a reasonable price.

The insight gained from the commonalities across these first-tier noncustomers shed light on how Pret could unlock and aggregate untapped demand. The Pret formula is simple. It offers restaurant-quality sandwiches made fresh every day from only the finest ingredients, and it makes the food available at a speed that is faster than that of restaurants and even fast food. It also delivers this in a sleek setting at reasonable prices.

Consider what Pret is like. Walking into a Pret A Manger is like walking into a bright Art Deco studio. Along the walls are clean refrigerated shelves stocked with more than thirty types of sandwiches (average price $4–$6) made fresh that day, in that shop, from fresh ingredients delivered earlier that morning. People can also choose from other freshly made items, such as salads, yogurt, parfaits, blended juices, and sushi. Each store has its own kitchen, and nonfresh items are made by high-quality producers. Even in its

New York stores, Pret's baguettes are from Paris, its croissants are from Belgium, and its Danish pastries are from Denmark. And nothing is kept over to the next day. Leftover food is given to homeless shelters.

In addition to offering fresh healthy sandwiches and other fresh food items, Pret speeds up the customer ordering experience from fast food's queue-order-pay-wait-receive-sit down purchasing cycle to a much faster browse-pick up-pay-leave cycle. On average, customers spend just ninety seconds from the time they get in line to the time they leave the shop. This is made possible because Pret produces ready-made sandwiches and other things at high volume with a high standardization of assembly, does not make to order, and does not serve its customers. They serve themselves as in a supermarket.

Whereas sit-down restaurants have seen stagnant demand, Pret has been converting the mass of soon-to-be noncustomers into core thriving customers who eat at Pret more often than they used to eat at restaurants. Beyond this, as with Callaway, restaurant-goers who were content to eat lunch at restaurants also have been flocking to Pret. Although restaurant lunches had been acceptable, the three key commonalities of first-tier noncustomers struck a chord with these people; but unlike soon-to-be noncustomers, they had not thought to question their lunch habits. The lesson: Noncustomers tend to offer far more insight into how to unlock and grow a blue ocean than do relatively content existing customers.

Today Pret A Manger sells more than twenty-five million sandwiches a year from its one hundred thirty stores in the U.K., and it recently opened stores in New York and Hong Kong. In 2002 it had sales of more than £100m ($160 million). Its growth potential triggered McDonald's to buy a 33 percent share of the company.

What are the key reasons first-tier noncustomers want to jump ship and leave your industry? Look for the commonalities across their responses. Focus on these, and not on the differences between them. You will glean insight into how to desegment buyers and unleash an ocean of latent untapped demand.

Second-Tier Noncustomers

These are *refusing* noncustomers, people who either do not use or cannot afford to use the current market offerings because they find the offerings unacceptable or beyond their means. Their needs are either dealt with by other means or ignored. Harboring within refusing noncustomers, however, is an ocean of untapped demand waiting to be released.

Consider how JCDecaux, a vendor of French outdoor advertising space, pulled the mass of refusing noncustomers into its market. Before JCDecaux created a new concept in outdoor advertising called "street furniture" in 1964, the outdoor advertising industry included billboards and transport advertisement. Billboards typically were located on city outskirts and along roads where traffic quickly passed by; transport advertisement comprised panels on buses and taxies, which again people caught sight of only as they whizzed by.

Outdoor advertising was not a popular campaign medium for many companies because it was viewed only in a transitory way. Outdoor ads were exposed to people for a very short time while they were in transit, and the rate of repeat visits was low. Especially for lesser-known companies, such advertising media were ineffective because they could not carry the comprehensive messages needed to introduce new names and products. Hence, many such companies refused to use such low-value-added outdoor advertising because it was either unacceptable or a luxury they could not afford.

Having thought through the key commonalities that cut across refusing noncustomers of the industry, JCDecaux realized that the lack of stationary downtown locations was the key reason the industry remained unpopular and small. In searching for a solution, JCDecaux found that municipalities could offer stationary downtown locations, such as bus stops, where people tended to wait a few minutes and hence had time to read and be influenced by advertisements. JCDecaux reasoned that if it could secure these locations to

use for outdoor advertising, it could convert second-tier noncustomers into customers.

This gave it the idea to provide street furniture, including maintenance and upkeep, free to municipalities. JCDecaux figured that
as long as the revenue generated from selling ad space exceeded the
costs of providing and maintaining the furniture at an attractive
profit margin, the company would be on a trajectory of strong, profitable growth. Accordingly, street furniture was created that would
integrate advertising panels.

In this way, JCDecaux created a breakthrough in value for second-tier noncustomers, the municipalities, and itself. The strategy
eliminated cities' traditional costs associated with urban furniture. In return for free products and services, JCDecaux gained the
exclusive right to display advertisements on the street furniture located in downtown areas. By making ads available in city centers,
the company significantly increased the average exposure time, improving the recall capabilities of this advertising medium. The increase in exposure time also permitted richer contents and more
complex messages. Moreover, as the maintainer of the urban furniture, JCDecaux could help advertisers roll out their campaigns in
two to three days, as opposed to fifteen days of rollout time for traditional billboard campaigns.

In response to JCDecaux's exceptional value offering, the mass
of refusing noncustomers flocked to the industry. As a medium of
advertisement, street furniture became the highest-growth market
in the overall display advertising industry. Global spending on
street furniture between 1995 and 2000, for example, grew by 60 percent compared with a 20 percent total increase in overall display
advertising.

By signing contracts of eight to twenty-five years with municipalities, JCDecaux gained long-term exclusive rights for displaying
ads with street furniture. After an initial capital investment, the
only expenditure for JCDecaux in the subsequent years was the
maintenance and renewal of the furniture. The operating margin
of street furniture was as high as 40 percent, compared with 14 per-

cent for billboards and 18 percent for transport advertisements. The exclusive contracts and high operating margins created a steady source of long-term revenue and profits. With this business model, JCDecaux was able to capture a leap in value for itself in return for a leap in value created for its buyers.

Today, JCDecaux is the number one street furniture-based ad space provider worldwide, with 283,000 panels in thirty-three countries. What's more, by looking to second-tier noncustomers and focusing on the key commonalities that turned them away from the industry, JCDecaux also increased the demand for outdoor advertising by existing customers of the industry. Until then, existing customers had focused on what billboard locations or bus lines they could secure, for what period, and for how much. They took for granted that those were the only options available and worked within them. Again, it took noncustomers to shed insight into the implicit assumptions of the industry and its existing customers that could be challenged and rewritten to create a leap in value for all.

What are the key reasons second-tier noncustomers refuse to use the products or services of your industry? Look for the commonalities across their responses. Focus on these, and not on their differences. You will glean insight into how to unleash an ocean of latent untapped demand.

Third-Tier Noncustomers

The third tier of noncustomers is the farthest away from an industry's existing customers. Typically, these *unexplored* noncustomers have not been targeted or thought of as potential customers by any player in the industry. That's because their needs and the business opportunities associated with them have somehow always been assumed to belong to other markets.

It would drive many companies crazy to know how many third-tier noncustomers they are forfeiting. Just think of the long-held assumption that tooth whitening was a service provided exclusively by dentists and not by oral care consumer-product companies. Consequently, oral care companies, until recently, never looked at the needs of these noncustomers. When they did, they found an ocean of latent demand waiting to be tapped; they also found that they had the capability to deliver safe, high-quality, low-cost tooth whitening solutions, and the market exploded.

This potential applies to most industries. Consider the U.S. defense aerospace industry. It has been argued that the inability to control aircraft costs is a key vulnerability in the long-term military strength of the United States.[1] Soaring costs combined with shrinking budgets, concluded a 1993 Pentagon report, left the military without a viable plan to replace its aging fleet of fighter aircraft.[2] If the military couldn't find a way to build aircraft differently, military leaders worried, the United States would not have enough airplanes to properly defend its interests.

Traditionally, the Navy, Marines, and Air Force differed in their conceptions of the ideal fighter plane and hence each branch designed and built its own aircraft independently. The Navy argued for a durable aircraft that would survive the stress of landing on carrier decks. The Marines wanted an expeditionary aircraft capable of short takeoffs and landings. The Air Force wanted the fastest and most sophisticated aircraft.

Historically, these differences among the independent branches were taken for granted, and the defense aerospace industry was regarded as having three distinct and separate segments. The Joint Strike Fighter (JSF) program challenged this industry practice.[3] It looked to all three segments as potentially unexplored noncustomers that could be aggregated into a new market of higher-performing, lower-cost fighter planes. Rather than accept the existing segmentation and develop products according to the differences in specifications and features demanded by each branch of the military, the JSF program questioned these differences. It searched for the key commonalities across the three branches that had previously disregarded one another.

This process revealed that the two highest-cost components of the three branches' aircraft were the same: avionics (software) and engines. The shared use and production of these components held the promise of enormous cost reductions. Moreover, even though each branch had a long list of highly customized requirements, most aircraft across branches performed the same missions.

The JSF team looked to understand how many of these highly customized features decisively influenced the branches' purchase decision. Interestingly, the Navy's answer did not hinge on a wide range of factors. Instead, it boiled down to only two: durability and maintainability. With aircraft stationed on aircraft carriers thousands of miles away from the nearest maintenance hangar, the Navy wants a fighter that is easy to maintain and yet durable as a Mack truck so that it can absorb the shock of carrier landings and constant exposure to salt air. Fearing that these two essential qualities would be compromised with the requirements of the Marines and the Air Force, the Navy bought its aircraft separately.

The Marines had many differences in requirements from those of the other branches, but again only two kept them from decisively avoiding joint aircraft purchases: the need for short takeoff vertical landing (STOVL) and robust countermeasures. To support troops in remote and hostile conditions the Marines need an aircraft that performs as a jet fighter and yet hovers like a helicopter. And given the low-altitude, expeditionary nature of their missions, the Marines want an aircraft equipped with various countermeasures—flares, electronic jamming devices—to evade enemy ground-to-air missiles because their planes are relatively easier targets given their short air-to-ground range.

Tasked with maintaining global air superiority, the Air Force demands the fastest aircraft and superior tactical agility—the ability to outmaneuver all current and future enemy aircraft—and one equipped with stealth technology: radar-absorbing materials and structures to make it less visible to radar and therefore more likely to evade enemy missiles and aircraft. The other two branches' aircraft lacked these factors, and hence the Air Force had not considered them.

These findings on unexplored noncustomers made the JSF a feasible project. The aim was to build one aircraft for all three divisions by combining those key factors while reducing or eliminating everything else—that is, all the factors that had been taken for granted by each branch but provided little value, or factors that had been overdesigned in the race to beat the competition. As outlined in figure 5-2, some twenty competing factors in the Marine, Navy, and Air Force segments were eliminated or reduced.

By combining the factors in this way and reducing or eliminating the rest, the JSF program is able to build one aircraft for all three branches. The result is a dramatic drop in costs and hence the price per aircraft, with a leap in value in performance for all three branches. Specifically, the JSF promised to reduce costs to $33 mil-

FIGURE 5-2

The Key Competing Factors of the Defense Aerospace Industry, After JSF

The JSF eliminated or reduced all existing competing factors other than those shaded.

Air Force	Navy	Marines	
Lightweight	Two engines	STOVL	Design customization
Integrated avionics	Two seats	Lightweight	
Stealth	Large wings	Short wings	
Supercruise engine	Durability	Countermeasures	
Long-distance	Long-distance		
Agility	Maintainability		
Air-air armaments	Large/flexible weapons payloads	Large/flexible weapons payloads	Weapons customization
Fixed internal weapons payload	Air-air and air-ground armaments	Air-ground armaments	
		Electronic warfare	
An aircraft built for every mission	An aircraft built for every mission	An aircraft built for every mission	Mission customization

lion per aircraft from the current $190 million. At the same time, the performance of the JSF, now called the F-35, promised to be superior to that of any of the top-performing aircraft for the three branches: the Air Force's F-22, the Marine's AV-8B Harrier jet, and the Navy's F-18. Figure 5-3 illustrates how the JSF creates exceptional value by offering superior performance at lower costs.

As revealed in the figure, the strategy canvas shows that while the JSF roughly maintains the distinctive strengths of the Air Force's aircraft—agility and stealth—it also offers greater maintainability, durability, countermeasures, and STOVL, the key strengths required by the Navy and the Marines. These factors are powerful additions that the Air Force had assumed it could not have. By focusing on these key decisive factors and dropping or reducing all other factors in the three dominant domains of customization—namely, design, weapons, and mission customization—the JSF program was able to offer a superior fighter plane at a lower cost.

FIGURE 5-3

Joint Strike Fighter (F-35) Versus Air Force F-22

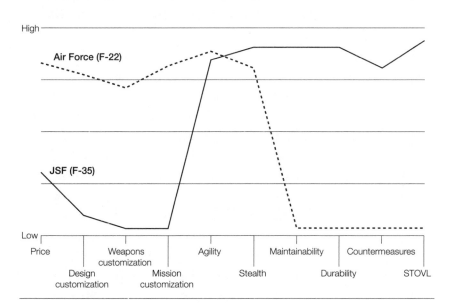

By reaching beyond the existing customers of each of the three military branches, the JSF aggregated demand previously divided among them. In fall 2001, Lockheed Martin was awarded the massive $200 billion JSF contract—the largest military contract in history—over Boeing. The first JSF F-35 is set to be delivered in 2010. To date, the Pentagon is confident that the program will be an unqualified success, not only because the strategic profile of the JSF F-35 achieves exceptional value but also, equally important, because it has won the support of all three defense branches.[4]

Go for the Biggest Catchment

There is no hard-and-fast rule to suggest which tier of noncustomers you should focus on and when. Because the scale of blue ocean opportunities that a specific tier of noncustomers can unlock varies across time and industries, you should focus on the tier that represents the biggest catchment at the time. But you should also explore whether there are overlapping commonalities across all three tiers of noncustomers. In that way, you can expand the scope of latent demand you can unleash. When that is the case, you should not focus on a specific tier but instead should look across tiers. The rule here is to go for the largest catchment.

The natural strategic orientation of many companies is toward retaining existing customers and seeking further segmentation opportunities. This is especially true in the face of competitive pressure. Although this might be a good way to gain a focused competitive advantage and increase share of the existing market space, it is not likely to produce a blue ocean that expands the market and creates new demand. The point here is not to argue that it's wrong to focus on existing customers or segmentation but rather to challenge these existing, taken-for-granted strategic orientations. What we suggest is that to maximize the scale of your blue ocean you should first reach beyond existing demand to noncustomers and desegmentation opportunities as you formulate future strategies.

If no such opportunities can be found, you can then move on to further exploit differences among existing customers. But in making such a strategic move, you should be aware that you might end up landing in a smaller space. You should also be aware that when your competitors succeed in attracting the mass of noncustomers with a value innovation move, many of your existing customers may be attracted away because they too may be willing to put their differences aside to gain the offered leap in value.

It is not enough to maximize the size of the blue ocean you are creating. You must profit from it to create a sustainable win-win outcome. The next chapter shows how to build a viable business model that produces and maintains profitable growth for your blue ocean offering.

~~~~~~

CHAPTER 6

Get the Strategic Sequence Right

YOU'VE LOOKED ACROSS PATHS to discover possible blue oceans. You've constructed a strategy canvas that clearly articulates your future blue ocean strategy. And you have explored how to aggregate the largest possible mass of buyers for your idea. The next challenge is to build a robust business model to ensure that you make a healthy profit on your blue ocean idea. This brings us to the fourth principle of blue ocean strategy: Get the strategic sequence right.

This chapter discusses the strategic sequence of fleshing out and validating blue ocean ideas to ensure their commercial viability. With an understanding of the right strategic sequence and of how to assess blue ocean ideas along the key criteria in that sequence, you dramatically reduce business model risk.

The Right Strategic Sequence

As shown in figure 6-1, companies need to build their blue ocean strategy in the sequence of buyer utility, price, cost, and adoption.

FIGURE 6-1

The Sequence of Blue Ocean Strategy

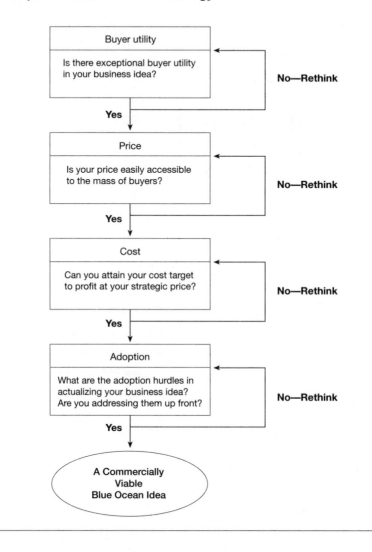

The starting point is buyer utility. Does your offering unlock exceptional utility? Is there a compelling reason for the mass of people to buy it? Absent this, there is no blue ocean potential to begin with. Here there are only two options. Park the idea, or rethink it until you reach an affirmative answer.

When you clear the exceptional utility bar, you advance to the second step: setting the right strategic price. Remember, a company does not want to rely solely on price to create demand. The key question here is this: Is your offering priced to attract the mass of target buyers so that they have a compelling ability to pay for your offering? If it is not, they cannot buy it. Nor will the offering create irresistible market buzz.

These first two steps address the revenue side of a company's business model. They ensure that you create a leap in net buyer value, where net buyer value equals the utility buyers receive minus the price they pay for it.

Securing the profit side brings us to the third element: cost. Can you produce your offering at the target cost and still earn a healthy profit margin? Can you profit at the strategic price—the price easily accessible to the mass of target buyers? You should not let costs drive prices. Nor should you scale down utility because high costs block your ability to profit at the strategic price. When the target cost cannot be met, you must either forgo the idea because the blue ocean won't be profitable, or you must innovate your business model to hit the target cost. The cost side of a company's business model ensures that it creates a leap in value for itself in the form of profit—that is, the price of the offering minus the cost of production. It is the combination of exceptional utility, strategic pricing, and target costing that allows companies to achieve value innovation—a leap in value for both buyers and companies.

The last step is to address adoption hurdles. What are the adoption hurdles in rolling out your idea? Have you addressed these up front? The formulation of blue ocean strategy is complete only when you can address adoption hurdles in the beginning to ensure the successful actualization of your idea. Adoption hurdles include, for example, potential resistance to the idea by retailers or partners. Because blue ocean strategies represent a significant departure from red oceans, it is key to address adoption hurdles up front.

How can you assess whether your blue ocean strategy is passing through each of the four sequential steps? And how can you refine your idea to pass each bar? Let's address these questions, starting with utility.

Testing for Exceptional Utility

The need to assess the buyer utility of your offering may seem self-evident. Yet many companies fail to deliver exceptional value because they are obsessed by the novelty of their product or service, especially if new technology plays a part in it.

Consider Philips' CD-i, an engineering marvel that failed to offer people a compelling reason to buy it. The player was promoted as the "Imagination Machine" because of its diverse functions. CD-i was a video machine, music system, game player, and teaching tool all wrapped into one. Yet it did so many different tasks that people could not understand how to use it. In addition, it lacked attractive software titles. So even though the CD-i theoretically could do almost anything, in reality it could do very little. Customers lacked a compelling reason to use it, and sales never took off.

Managers responsible for Philips' CD-i (as well as Motorola's Iridium) fell into the same trap: They reveled in the bells and whistles of their new technology. They acted on the assumption that bleeding-edge technology is equivalent to bleeding-edge utility for buyers—something that, our research found, is rarely the case.

The technology trap that snagged Philips and Motorola trips up the best and brightest companies time and again. Unless the technology makes buyers' lives dramatically simpler, more convenient, more productive, less risky, or more fun and fashionable, it will not attract the masses no matter how many awards it wins. Think, for example, of Starbucks, Cirque du Soleil, The Home Depot, Southwest Airlines, [yellow tail], or Ralph Lauren: Value innovation is not the same as technology innovation.

To get around this trap, the starting point, as articulated in chapter 2, is to create a strategic profile that passes the initial litmus test of being focused, being divergent, and having a compelling tagline that speaks to buyers. Having done this, companies are ready to expressly assess where and how the new product or service will change the lives of its buyers. Such a difference in perspective is important because it means that the way a product or service is developed becomes less a function of its technical possibilities and more a function of its utility to buyers.

The buyer utility map helps managers look at this issue from the right perspective (see figure 6-2). It outlines all the levers companies can pull to deliver exceptional utility to buyers as well as the various experiences buyers can have with a product or service. This map allows managers to identify the full range of utility spaces that a product or service can potentially fill. Let's look at the map's dimensions in detail.

FIGURE 6-2

The Buyer Utility Map

	The Six Stages of the Buyer Experience Cycle					
	1. Purchase	2. Delivery	3. Use	4. Supplements	5. Maintenance	6. Disposal
Customer productivity						
Simplicity						
Convenience						
Risk						
Fun and image						
Environmental friendliness						

The Six Utility Levers

The Six Stages of the Buyer Experience Cycle

A buyer's experience can usually be broken into a cycle of six stages, running more or less sequentially from purchase to disposal. Each stage encompasses a wide variety of specific experiences. Purchasing, for example, may include the experience of browsing eBay as well as the aisles of The Home Depot. At each stage, managers can ask a set of questions to gauge the quality of buyers' experience, as described in figure 6-3.

The Six Utility Levers

Cutting across the stages of the buyer's experience are what we call *utility levers*: the ways in which companies can unlock exceptional utility for buyers. Most of the levers are obvious. Simplicity, fun and image, and environmental friendliness need little explanation. Nor does the idea that a product might reduce a customer's financial, physical, or credibility risks. And a product or service offers convenience simply by being easy to obtain, use, or dispose of. The most commonly used lever is that of customer productivity, in which an offering helps a customer do things faster or better.

To test for exceptional utility, companies should check whether their offering has removed the greatest blocks to utility across the entire buyer experience cycle for customers and noncustomers. The greatest blocks to utility often represent the greatest and most pressing opportunities to unlock exceptional value. Figure 6-4 shows how a company can identify the most compelling hot spots to unlock exceptional utility. By locating your proposed offering on the thirty-six spaces of the buyer utility map, you can clearly see how, and whether, the new idea not only creates a different utility proposition from existing offerings but also removes the biggest blocks to utility that stand in the way of converting noncustomers into customers. If your offering falls on the same space or spaces as those of other players, chances are it is not a blue ocean offering.

FIGURE 6-3

The Buyer Experience Cycle

Purchase →	Delivery →	Use →	Supplements →	Maintenance →	Disposal
How long does it take to find the product you need?	How long does it take to get the product delivered?	Does the product require training or expert assistance?	Do you need other products and services to make this product work?	Does the product require external maintenance?	Does use of the product create waste items?
Is the place of purchase attractive and accessible?	How difficult is it to unpack and install the new product?	Is the product easy to store when not in use?	If so, how costly are they?	How easy is it to maintain and upgrade the product?	How easy is it to dispose of the product?
How secure is the transaction environment?	Do buyers have to arrange delivery themselves? If yes, how costly and difficult is this?	How effective are the product's features and functions?	How much time do they take?	How costly is maintenance?	Are there legal or environmental issues in disposing of the product safely?
How rapidly can you make a purchase?		Does the product or service deliver far more power or options than required by the average user? Is it overcharged with bells and whistles?	How much pain do they cause?		How costly is disposal?
			How easy are they to obtain?		

FIGURE 6-4

Uncovering the Blocks to Buyer Utility

Purchase	Delivery	Use	Supplements	Maintenance	Disposal
Customer Productivity:		In which stage are the biggest blocks to customer productivity?			
Simplicity:		In which stage are the biggest blocks to simplicity?			
Convenience:		In which stage are the biggest blocks to convenience?			
Risk:		In which stage are the biggest blocks to reducing risks?			
Fun and Image:		In which stage are the biggest blocks to fun and image?			
Environmental Friendliness:		In which stage are the biggest blocks to environmental friendliness?			

Consider the Ford Model T. Before its debut, the more than five hundred automakers in the United States focused on building custom-made luxury autos for the wealthy. In terms of the buyer utility map, the entire industry focused on image in the use phase, creating luxury cars for fashionable weekend outings. Only one of the thirty-six utility spaces was occupied.

The greatest blocks to utility for the mass of people, however, were not in refining the auto's luxury or stylish image. Rather, they had to do with two other factors. One was convenience in the use phase. The bumpy and muddy dirt roads that prevailed at the century's start were a natural for horses to tread over but often prevented finely crafted autos from passing. This significantly limited where and when cars could travel (driving on rainy and snowy days was ill advised), making the use of the car limited and inconvenient. The second block to utility was risk in the maintenance phase. The cars, being finely crafted and having multiple options, often broke down, requiring experts to fix them, and experts were expensive and in short supply.

In one fell swoop, Ford's Model T eliminated these two utility blocks. The Model T was called the car for the great multitude. It came in only one color (black) and one model, with scant options. In this way, Ford eliminated investments in image in the use phase. Instead of creating cars for weekends in the countryside—a luxury few could justify—Ford's Model T was made for everyday use. It was reliable. It was durable; it was designed to travel effortlessly over dirt roads and in rain, sleet, or shine. It was easy to fix and use. People could learn to drive it in one day.

In this way the buyer utility map highlights the differences between ideas that genuinely create new and exceptional utility and those that are essentially revisions of existing offerings or technological breakthroughs not linked to value. The aim is to check whether your offering passes the exceptional utility test, as did the Model T. By applying this diagnostic, you can find out how your idea needs to be refined.

Where are the greatest blocks to utility across the buyer experience cycle for your customers and noncustomers? Does your offering effectively eliminate these blocks? If it does not, chances are your offering is innovation for innovation's sake or a revision of existing offerings. When a company's offering passes this test, it is ready to move to the next step.

From Exceptional Utility to Strategic Pricing

To secure a strong revenue stream for your offering, you must set the right strategic price. This step ensures that buyers not only will want to buy your offering but also will have a compelling ability to pay for it. Many companies take a reverse course, first testing the waters of a new product or service by targeting novelty-seeking, price-insensitive customers at the launch of a new business idea; only over time do they drop prices to attract mainstream buyers. It is increasingly important, however, to know from the start what price will quickly capture the mass of target buyers.

There are two reasons for this change. First, companies are discovering that volume generates higher returns than it used to. As the nature of goods becomes more knowledge intensive, companies bear much more of their costs in product development than in manufacturing. This is easy to understand in the software industry. Producing the first copy of the Windows XP operating system, for example, cost Microsoft billions of dollars, whereas subsequent copies involved no more than the nearly trivial cost of a CD. This makes volume key.

A second reason is that to a buyer, the value of a product or service may be closely tied to the total number of people using it. An example is the online auction service managed by eBay. People will not buy a product or service when it is used by few others. As a result of this phenomenon, called *network externalities*, many products and services are an all-or-nothing proposition: Either you sell millions at once, or you sell nothing at all.[1]

In the meantime, the rise of knowledge-intensive products also creates the potential for free riding. This relates to the nonrival and partially excludable nature of knowledge.[2] The use of a *rival good* by one firm precludes its use by another. So, for example, Nobel Prize–winning scientists who are fully employed by IBM cannot simultaneously be employed by another company. Nor can scrap steel consumed by Nucor be simultaneously consumed for production by other minimill steel makers.

In contrast, the use of a *nonrival good* by one firm does not limit its use by another. Ideas fall into this category. So, for example, when Virgin Atlantic Airways launched its Upper Class brand—a new concept in business-class travel that essentially combined the huge seats and legroom of traditional first class with the price of business-class tickets—other airlines were free to apply this idea to their own business-class service without limiting Virgin's ability to use it. This makes competitive imitation not only possible but less costly. The cost and risk of developing an innovative idea are borne by the initiator, not the follower.

This challenge is exacerbated when the notion of *excludability* is considered. Excludability is a function both of the nature of the good and of the legal system. A good is excludable if the company can prevent others from using it because of, for example, limited access or patent protection. Intel, for example, can exclude other microprocessor chipmakers from using its manufacturing facilities through property ownership laws. The women's fitness club Curves, however, cannot exclude someone from walking into any of its centers, studying its layout, atmosphere, and exercise routine, and mimicking its women's fitness concept: Women need only thirty minutes, three days a week, to get in shape while having fun with other women, with none of the usual embarrassment faced at gyms. The highest value-added element of the Curves formula is not excludable. Once ideas are out there, knowledge naturally spills over to other firms.

This lack of excludability reinforces the risk of free riding. Like the creative and explosive concepts of Curves, Starbucks, or Southwest Airlines, many of the most powerful blue ocean ideas have tremendous value but in themselves consist of no new technological discoveries. As a result they are neither patentable nor excludable and hence are vulnerable to imitation.

All this means that the strategic price you set for your offering must not only attract buyers in large numbers but also help you to retain them. Given the high potential for free riding, an offering's reputation must be earned on day one, because brand building increasingly relies heavily on word-of-mouth recommendations spreading rapidly through our networked society. Companies must therefore start with an offer that buyers can't refuse and must keep it that way to discourage any free-riding imitations. This is what makes strategic pricing key. Strategic pricing addresses this question: Is your offering priced to attract the mass of target buyers from the start so that they have a compelling ability to pay for it? When exceptional utility is combined with strategic pricing, imitation is discouraged.

We have developed a tool called the *price corridor of the mass* to help managers find the right price for an irresistible offer, which, by the way, isn't necessarily the lower price. The tool involves two distinct but interrelated steps (see figure 6-5).

FIGURE 6-5

The Price Corridor of the Mass

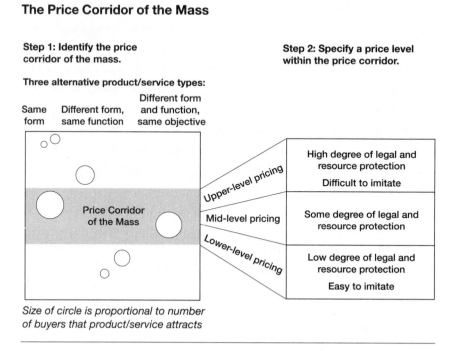

Size of circle is proportional to number
of buyers that product/service attracts

Step 1: Identify the Price Corridor of the Mass

In setting a price, all companies look first at the products and services that most closely resemble their idea in terms of form. Typically
they look at other products and services within their industries.
That's still a necessary exercise, of course, but it is not sufficient to
attract new customers. So the main challenge in determining a
strategic price is to understand the price sensitivities of those people who will be comparing the new product or service with a host of
very different-looking products and services offered outside the
group of traditional competitors.

A good way to look outside industry boundaries is to list products and services that fall into two categories: those that take different forms but perform the same function, and those that take different
forms and functions but share the same over-arching objective.

Different form, same function. Many companies that create blue oceans attract customers from other industries who use a product or service that performs the same function or bears the same core utility as the new one but takes a very different physical form. In the case of Ford's Model T, Ford looked to the horse-drawn carriage. The horse-drawn carriage had the same core utility as the car: transportation for individuals and families. But it had a very different form: a live animal versus a machine. Ford effectively converted the majority of noncustomers of the auto industry, namely customers of horse-drawn carriages, into customers of its own blue ocean by pricing its Model T against horse-drawn carriages and not the cars of other automakers.

In the case of the school lunch catering industry, raising this question led to an interesting insight. Suddenly those parents who make their children's lunches came into the equation. For many children, parents had the same function: making their child's lunch. But they had a very different form: mom or dad versus a lunch line in the cafeteria.

Different form and function, same objective. Some companies lure customers from even further away. Cirque du Soleil, for example, has diverted customers from a wide range of evening activities. Its growth came in part through drawing people away from other activities that differed in both form and function. For example, bars and restaurants have few physical features in common with a circus. They also serve a distinct function by providing conversational and gastronomical pleasure, a very different experience from the visual entertainment that a circus offers. Yet despite these differences in form and function, people have the same objective in undertaking these three activities: to enjoy a night out.

Listing the groups of alternative products and services allows managers to see the full range of buyers they can poach from other industries as well as from nonindustries, such as parents (for the school lunch catering industry) or the noble pencil in managing household finances (for the personal finance software industry).

Having done this, managers should then graphically plot the price and volume of these alternatives, as shown in figure 6-5.

This approach provides a straightforward way to identify where the mass of target buyers is and what prices these buyers are prepared to pay for the products and services they currently use. The price bandwidth that captures the largest groups of target buyers is the price corridor of the mass.

In some cases, the range is very wide. For Southwest Airlines, for example, the price corridor of the mass covered the group of people paying, on average, $400 to buy an economy-class short-haul ticket to about $60 for the cost of going the same distance by car. The key here is not to pursue pricing against the competition within an industry but rather to pursue pricing against substitutes and alternatives across industries and nonindustries. Had Ford, for example, priced its Model T against other autos, which were more than three times the price of horse-drawn carriages, the market for the Model T would not have exploded.

Step 2: Specify a Level Within the Price Corridor

The second part of the tool helps managers determine how high a price they can afford to set within the corridor without inviting competition from imitation products or services. That assessment depends on two principal factors. First is the degree to which the product or service is protected legally through patents or copyrights. Second is the degree to which the company owns some exclusive asset or core capability, such as an expensive production plant, that can block imitation. Dyson, a British electrical white goods company, for example, has been able to charge a high unit price for its bagless vacuum cleaner since the product's launch in 1995, thanks to both strong patents and hard-to-imitate service capabilities.

Many other companies have used upper-boundary strategic pricing to attract the mass of target buyers. Examples include DuPont with its Lycra brand in specialty chemicals, Philips' ALTO in the professional lighting industry, SAP in the business application software industry, and Bloomberg in the financial software industry.

On the other hand, companies with uncertain patent and asset protection should consider pricing somewhere in the middle of the corridor. As for companies that have no such protection, they must set a relatively low price. In the case of Southwest Airlines, because its service wasn't patentable and required no exclusive assets, its ticket prices fell into the lower boundary of the corridor—namely, against the price of car travel. Companies would be wise to pursue mid- to lower-boundary strategic pricing from the start if any of the following apply:

- Their blue ocean offering has high fixed costs and marginal variable costs.

- Their attractiveness depends heavily on network externalities.

- Their cost structure benefits from steep economies of scale and scope. In these cases, volume brings with it significant cost advantages, something that makes pricing for volume even more key.

The price corridor of the mass not only signals the strategic pricing zone central to pulling in an ocean of new demand but also signals how you might need to adjust your initial price estimates to achieve this. When your offering passes the test of strategic pricing, you're ready to move to the next step.

From Strategic Pricing to Target Costing

Target costing, the next step in the strategic sequence, addresses the profit side of the business model. To maximize the profit potential of a blue ocean idea, a company should start with the strategic price and then deduct its desired profit margin from the price to arrive at the target cost. Here, price-minus costing, and not cost-plus pricing, is essential if you are to arrive at a cost structure that is both profitable and hard for potential followers to match.

When target costing is driven by strategic pricing, however, it is usually aggressive. Part of the challenge of meeting the target cost is addressed in building a strategic profile that has not only divergence but also focus, which makes a company strip out costs. Think of the cost reductions Cirque du Soleil enjoyed by eliminating animals and stars or that Ford enjoyed by making the Model T in one color and one model having few options.

Sometimes these reductions are sufficient to hit the cost target, but often they are not. Consider the cost innovations that Ford had to introduce to meet its aggressive target cost for the Model T. Ford had to scrap the standard manufacturing system, in which cars were handmade by skilled craftsmen from start to finish. Instead, Ford introduced the assembly line, which replaced skilled craftsmen with ordinary unskilled laborers, who worked one small task faster and more efficiently, cutting the time to make a Model T from twenty-one days to four days and cutting labor hours by 60 percent.[3] Had Ford not introduced these cost innovations, it could not have met its strategic price profitably.

Instead of drilling down and finding ways to creatively meet the target cost as Ford did, if companies give in to the tempting route of either bumping up the strategic price or cutting back on utility, they are not on the path to lucrative blue waters. To hit the cost target, companies have three principal levers.

The first involves streamlining operations and introducing cost innovations from manufacturing to distribution. Can the product's or service's raw materials be replaced by unconventional, less expensive ones—such as switching from metal to plastic or shifting a call center from the U.K. to Bangalore? Can high-cost, low-value-added activities in your value chain be significantly eliminated, reduced, or outsourced? Can the physical location of your product or service be shifted from prime real estate locations to lower-cost locations, as The Home Depot, IKEA, and Wal-Mart have done in retail or Southwest Airlines has done by shifting from major to secondary airports? Can you truncate the number of parts or steps used in production by shifting the way things are made, as Ford did by introducing the assembly line? Can you digitize activities to reduce costs?

By probing questions such as these, the Swiss watch company Swatch, for example, was able to arrive at a cost structure some 30 percent lower than any other watch company in the world. At the start, Nicolas Hayek, chairman of Swatch, set up a project team to determine the strategic price for the Swatch. At the time, cheap (about $75), high-precision quartz watches from Japan and Hong Kong were capturing the mass market. Swatch set the price at $40, a price at which people could buy multiple Swatches as fashion accessories. The low price left no profit margin for Japanese or Hong Kong-based companies to copy Swatch and undercut its price. Directed to sell the Swatch for that price and not a penny more, the Swatch project team worked backwards to arrive at the target cost, a process that involved determining the margin Swatch needed to support marketing and services and earn a profit.

Given the high cost of Swiss labor, Swatch was able to achieve this goal only by making radical changes in the product and production methods. Instead of using the more traditional metal or leather, for example, Swatch used plastic. Swatch's engineers also drastically simplified the design of the watch's inner workings, reducing the number of parts from one hundred fifty to fifty-one. Finally, the engineers developed new and cheaper assembly techniques; for example, the watch cases were sealed by ultrasonic welding instead of screws. Taken together, the design and manufacturing changes enabled Swatch to reduce direct labor costs from 30 percent to less than 10 percent of total costs. These cost innovations produced a cost structure that is hard to beat and let Swatch profitably dominate the mass market for watches, a market previously dominated by Asian manufacturers with a cheaper labor pool.

Beyond streamlining operations and introducing cost innovations, a second lever companies can pull to meet their target cost is partnering. In bringing a new product or service to market, many companies mistakenly try to carry out all the production and distribution activities themselves. Sometimes that's because they see the product or service as a platform for developing new capabilities. Other times it is simply a matter of not considering other outside options. Partnering, however, provides a way for companies to secure needed capabilities fast and effectively while dropping their cost structure. It allows a company to leverage other companies' expertise and economies of scale. Partnering includes closing gaps in capabilities through making small acquisitions when doing so is faster and cheaper, providing access to needed expertise that has already been mastered.

A large part of IKEA's ability to meet its target cost, for example, comes down to partnering. IKEA seeks out the lowest prices for materials and production via partnering with some fifteen hundred manufacturing companies in more than fifty countries to ensure it the lowest cost and fastest production of products in its IKEA lineup of some twenty thousand items.

Or consider German-based, world-leading business application software maker SAP. By partnering with Oracle, SAP saved hundreds of millions if not billions of dollars in development costs and got a world-class central database, namely Oracle's, which sits at the heart of SAP's core products R/2 and R/3. SAP went a step further and also partnered with leading consulting firms, such as Capgemini and Accenture, to gain a global sales force overnight at no extra cost. Whereas Oracle had the fixed costs of a much smaller sales force on its balance sheet, SAP was able to leverage Capgemini's and Accenture's strong global networks to reach SAP's target customers, with no cost implication to the company.

Sometimes, however, no amount of streamlining and cost innovation or partnering will make it possible for a company to deliver its target cost. This brings us to the third lever companies can use to make their desired profit margin without compromising their strategic price: changing the pricing model of the industry. By changing the pricing model used—and not the level of the strategic price—companies can often overcome this problem.

When film videotapes first came out, for example, they were priced at around $80. Few people were willing to pay that amount because no one expected to watch the video more than two or three times. The strategic price of a video had to be set in relation to going to the movies and not to owning a tape for life. So at $80 a tape, demand was not taking off. How could a company make money by selling the videos at only a few dollars if it followed the path of using strategic pricing? The answer was that it couldn't. Blockbuster, however, got around this problem by changing the pricing model from selling to renting. This allowed it to strategically price videotapes at only a few dollars per rental. The result was that the home video market exploded and Blockbuster made more money by repeatedly renting the same $80 videos than it could have by selling them outright. Similarly, IBM exploded the tabulating market by shifting the pricing model from selling to leasing to hit its strategic price while covering its cost structure.

In addition to Blockbuster's rental model or IBM's leasing model, companies have used several innovations in pricing models to profitably deliver on the strategic price. One model is the *time-share*. The New Jersey company NetJets follows this model to make jets accessible to a wide range of corporate customers, who buy the right to use a jet for a certain amount of time rather than buy the jet itself. Another model is the *slice-share*; mutual fund managers, for example, bring high-quality portfolio services—traditionally provided by private banks to the rich—to the small investor by selling a sliver of the portfolio rather than its whole.

Some companies are abandoning the concept of price altogether. Instead, they give products to customers in return for an *equity interest* in the customer's business. Hewlett-Packard, for example, has traded high-powered servers to Silicon Valley start-ups for a share of their revenues. The customers get immediate access to a key capability, and HP stands to earn a lot more than the price of the machine. The aim is not to compromise on the strategic price but to hit the target through a new price model. We call this *pricing innovation*. Remember, however, that what is a pricing innovation for one industry, such as video rentals, is often a standard pricing model in another industry.

Figure 6-6 shows how value innovation typically maximizes profit by using the foregoing three levers. As the figure depicts, a

FIGURE 6-6

The Profit Model of Blue Ocean Strategy

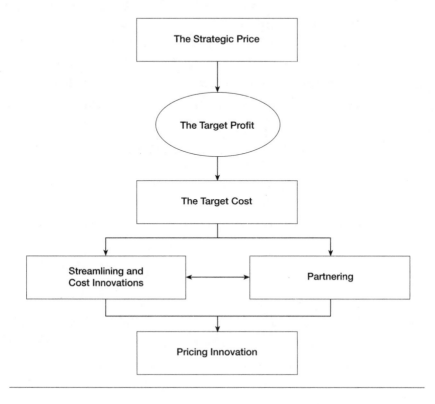

company begins with its strategic price, from which it deducts its target profit margin to arrive at its target cost. To hit the cost target that supports that profit, companies have two key levers: One is streamlining and cost innovations, and the other is partnering. When the target cost cannot be met despite all efforts to build a low-cost business model, the company should turn to the third lever, pricing innovation, to profitably meet the strategic price. Of course, even when the target cost can be met, pricing innovation still can be pursued. When a company's offering successfully addresses the profit side of the business model, the company is ready to advance to the final step in the sequence of blue ocean strategy.

A business model built in the sequence of exceptional utility, strategic pricing, and target costing produces value innovation. Unlike the practice of conventional technology innovators, value innovation is based on a win-win game among buyers, companies, and society. Appendix C, "The Market Dynamics of Value Innovation," illustrates how such a game is played out in the market and shows the economic and social welfare implications for its stakeholders.

From Utility, Price, and Cost to Adoption

Even an unbeatable business model may not be enough to guarantee the commercial success of a blue ocean idea. Almost by definition, it threatens the status quo, and for that reason it may provoke fear and resistance among a company's three main stakeholders: its employees, its business partners, and the general public. Before plowing forward and investing in the new idea, the company must first overcome such fears by educating the fearful.

Employees

Failure to adequately address the concerns of employees about the impact of a new business idea on their livelihoods can be expensive. When Merrill Lynch's management, for example, announced plans to create an online brokerage service, its stock price fell by 14 percent as reports emerged of resistance and infighting within the company's large retail brokerage division.

Before companies go public with an idea, they should make a concerted effort to communicate to employees that they are aware of the threats posed by the execution of the idea. Companies should work with employees to find ways of defusing the threats so that everyone in the company wins, despite shifts in people's roles, responsibilities, and rewards. In contrast to Merrill Lynch, Morgan Stanley Dean Witter & Co. engaged employees in an open internal discussion of the company's strategy for meeting the challenge of the Internet. Morgan's efforts paid off handsomely. Because the market realized that its employees understood the need for an e-venture, the company's shares rose 13 percent when it eventually announced the venture.

Business Partners

Potentially even more damaging than employee disaffection is the resistance of partners who fear that their revenue streams or market positions are threatened by a new business idea. That was the problem faced by SAP when it was developing its product AcceleratedSAP (ASAP), an enterprise software system that was fast to implement and hence low cost. ASAP brought business application software within the reach of midsized and small companies for the first time. The problem was that the development of best-practice templates for ASAP required the active cooperation of large consulting firms that were deriving substantial income from lengthy implementations of SAP's other products. As a result, they were not necessarily incentivized to find the fastest way to implement the company's software.

SAP resolved the dilemma by openly discussing the issues with its partners. Its executives convinced the consulting firms that they stood to gain more business by cooperating. Although ASAP would reduce implementation time for small and midsized companies, consultants would gain access to a new client base that would more than compensate for some lost revenues from larger companies. The new system would also offer consultants a way to respond to customers' increasingly vocal concerns that business application software took too long to implement.

The General Public

Opposition to a new business idea can also spread to the general public, especially if the idea is very new and innovative, threatening established social or political norms. The effects can be devastating. Consider Monsanto, which makes genetically modified foods. Its intentions have been questioned by European consumers, largely because of the efforts of environmental groups such as Greenpeace, Friends of the Earth, and the Soil Association. The attacks of these groups have struck many chords in Europe, which has a history of environmental concern and powerful agricultural lobbies.

Monsanto's mistake was to let others take charge of the debate. The company should have educated the environmental groups as well as the public on the benefits of genetically modified food and its potential to eliminate world famine and disease. When the products came out, Monsanto should have given consumers a choice between organic and genetically modified foods by labeling which products had genetically modified seeds as their base. If Monsanto had taken these steps, then instead of being vilified, it might have ended up as the "Intel Inside" of food for the future—the provider of the essential technology.

In educating these three groups of stakeholders—your employees, your partners, and the general public—the key challenge is to engage in an open discussion about why the adoption of the new idea is necessary. You need to explain its merits, set clear expectations for its ramifications, and describe how the company will address them. Stakeholders need to know that their voices have been heard and that there will be no surprises. Companies that take the trouble to have such a dialogue with stakeholders will find that it amply repays the time and effort involved. (For a fuller discussion of how companies can engage stakeholders, see chapter 8.)

The Blue Ocean Idea Index

Although companies should build their blue ocean strategy in the sequence of utility, price, cost, and adoption, these criteria form an integral whole to ensure commercial success. The *blue ocean idea* (BOI) *index* provides a simple but robust test of this system view (see Figure 6-7).

FIGURE 6-7

Blue Ocean Idea (BOI) Index

		Philips CD-i	Motorola Iridium	DoCoMo i-mode Japan
Utility	Is there exceptional utility? Are there compelling reasons to buy your offering?	–	–	+
Price	Is your price easily accessible to the mass of buyers?	–	–	+
Cost	Does your cost structure meet the target cost?	–	–	+
Adoption	Have you addressed adoption hurdles up front?	–	+/–	+

As shown in figure 6-7, had Philips' CD-i and Motorola's Iridium scored their ideas on the BOI index they would have seen how far they were from opening up lucrative blue oceans. With respect to Philips CD-i, it did not create exceptional buyer utility with its offering of complex technological functions and limited software titles. It was priced out of reach of the mass of buyers, and its manufacturing process was complicated and costly. With its complicated design, it took more than thirty minutes to explain and sell to customers, something that gave no incentive for sales clerks to sell CD-i in fast-moving retail. Philips CD-i therefore failed all four criteria on the BOI index despite the billions poured into it.

By assessing the business idea of the CD-i against the BOI index during development, Philips could have foreseen the shortcomings embedded in the idea and addressed them up front by simplifying the product and locking in partners to develop winning software titles, setting a strategic price accessible to the masses, instituting price-minus costing instead of cost-plus pricing, and working with retail to find a simple, easy way for the sales force to sell and explain the product in a few minutes.

Similarly, Motorola's Iridium was unreasonably expensive because of high production costs. It provided no attractive utility for the mass of buyers, not being usable in buildings or cars and being the size of a brick. When it came to adoption, Motorola overcame many regulations and secured transmission rights from numerous countries. Employees, partners, and the society were also reasonably motivated to accept the idea. But the company had a weak sales team and marketing channels in the global markets. Because Motorola was not able to follow up sales leads effectively, Iridium phone sets were sometimes unavailable when requested. Weak utility, price, and cost positions, plus average adoption ability, indicated that the Iridium idea would be a flop.

In contrast to these failures, consider NTT DoCoMo's i-mode launch in Japan. In 1999, when most telecom operators were focusing on technology races and price competition over voice-based wireless devices, NTT DoCoMo, the largest Japanese telecom operator, launched i-mode to offer the Internet on cell phones. Regular mobile telephony in Japan had reached a high level of sophistication in terms of mobility, quality of voice, ease of use, and hardware design. But it offered few data-based services such as e-mail, access to information, news, and games, and transaction capabilities, which were the killer applications of the PC-Internet world. The i-mode service brought together the key advantages of these two alternative industries—the cell phone industry and the PC-Internet industry—and created unique and superior buyer utility.

The i-mode service offered exceptional buyer utility at a price accessible to the mass of buyers. The monthly i-mode subscription fee, the voice and data transmission fee, and the price of content were in the "nonreflection" strategic price zone, encouraging impulse buying and reaching the masses as quickly as possible. For example, the monthly subscription fee for a content site is between ¥100 and ¥300 ($1 and $3), which is the result of benchmarking against the price of the weekly magazines most Japanese regularly pick up at their train station kiosk.

After setting a price that was attractive to the mass of buyers, NTT DoCoMo strove to obtain the capabilities it needed to deliver the service within its cost target in order to turn a profit. In achieving this end, the company was never bounded by its own assets and capabilities. While it focused on its traditional role as an operator to develop and maintain a high-speed, high-capacity network in the i-mode project, it sought to deliver other key elements of its offering by actively partnering with handset manufacturers and information providers.

By creating a win-win partnership network, the company aimed to meet and sustain the target cost set by its strategic price. Although there are many partners and dimensions involved in its partnership network, a few aspects are particularly relevant here. First, NTT DoCoMo regularly and persistently shared know-how and technology with its handset manufacturing partners to help them stay ahead of their competitors. Second, the company played the role of the portal and gateway to the wireless network, expanding and updating the list of i-mode menu sites while attracting content providers to join the i-mode list and create the content that would boost user traffic. By handling the billing for the content providers with a small commission fee, for example, the company offered content providers major cost savings associated with billing system development. At the same time DoCoMo also obtained a growing revenue stream for itself.

More importantly, instead of using the Wireless Markup Language (WML) under the WAP standard for site creation, i-mode used c-HTML, an existing and already widely used language in Japan. This made i-mode more attractive to content providers because under c-HTML, software engineers needed no retraining to convert their existing Web sites, designed for the Internet environment, into sites for i-mode use, and thus they incurred no additional costs. NTT DoCoMo also entered into collaborative arrangements with key foreign partners, such as Sun Microsystems, Microsoft, and Symbian, to reduce the total development costs and shorten the time for an effective launch.

Another key aspect of the i-mode strategy was the way the project was carried out. A team specially dedicated to the project was set up and given a clear mandate and autonomy. The head of the i-mode team selected most of the team members and engaged them in an open discussion on how to create the new market of mobile data communications, making them committed to the project. All this created a favorable corporate environment for the adoption of i-mode. Moreover, the win-win game the company created for its partners, as well as the readiness of the Japanese general public to use database services, also contributed to the successful adoption of i-mode.

The i-mode service passed all four criteria on the BOI index, as shown earlier in figure 6-7. Indeed, i-mode turned out to be an explosive success. Six months after its launch, subscribers had reached the 1 million mark. Within two years, the number of subscribers had reached 21.7 million, and revenues from packet transmission alone had increased 130 times. By the end of 2003 the number of subscribers had reached 40.1 million, and revenues from the transmission of data, pictures, and text increased from 295 million yen ($2.6 million) to 886.3 billion yen ($8 billion).

DoCoMo is the only company that has been able to make money out of the mobile Internet. DoCoMo now exceeds its parent company, NTT, in terms of market capitalization as well as potential for profitable growth.

Although i-mode has been a huge success in Japan, its success outside Japan hinges on whether it can overcome regional adoption barriers of a regulatory, cultural, and emotional nature as well as those stemming from partnership dynamics and infrastructure economics.

Having passed the blue ocean idea index, companies are ready to shift gears from the formulation side of blue ocean strategy to its execution. The question is, How do you bring an organization with you to execute this strategy even though it often represents a significant departure from the past? This brings us to the second part of this book, and the fifth principle of blue ocean strategy: overcoming key organizational hurdles, the subject of our next chapter.

PART THREE

Executing Blue Ocean Strategy

CHAPTER 7

Overcome Key
Organizational Hurdles

O NCE A COMPANY HAS DEVELOPED a blue ocean strategy with a profitable business model, it must execute it. The challenge of execution exists, of course, for any strategy. Companies, like individuals, often have a tough time translating thought into action whether in red or blue oceans. But compared with red ocean strategy, blue ocean strategy represents a significant departure from the status quo. It hinges on a shift from convergence to divergence in value curves at lower costs. That raises the execution bar.

Managers have assured us that the challenge is steep. They face four hurdles. One is cognitive: waking employees up to the need for a strategic shift. Red oceans may not be the paths to future profitable growth, but they feel comfortable to people and may have even served an organization well until now, so why rock the boat?

The second hurdle is limited resources. The greater the shift in strategy, the greater it is assumed are the resources needed to execute it. But resources were being cut, and not raised, in many of the organizations we studied.

Third is motivation. How do you motivate key players to move fast and tenaciously to carry out a break from the status quo? That will take years, and managers don't have that kind of time.

The final hurdle is politics. As one manager put it, "In our organization you get shot down before you stand up."

Although all companies face different degrees of these hurdles, and many may face only some subset of the four, knowing how to triumph over them is key to attenuating organizational risk. This brings us to the fifth principle of blue ocean strategy: Overcome key organizational hurdles to make blue ocean strategy happen in action.

To achieve this effectively, however, companies must abandon perceived wisdom on effecting change. Conventional wisdom asserts that the greater the change, the greater the resources and time you will need to bring about results. Instead, you need to flip conventional wisdom on its head using what we call *tipping point leadership*. Tipping point leadership allows you to overcome these four hurdles fast and at low cost while winning employees' backing in executing a break from the status quo.

Tipping Point Leadership in Action

Consider the New York City Police Department (NYPD), which executed a blue ocean strategy in the 1990s in the public sector. When Bill Bratton was appointed police commissioner of New York City in February 1994, the odds were stacked against him to an extent few executives ever face. In the early 1990s, New York City was veering toward anarchy. Murders were at an all-time high. Muggings, Mafia hits, vigilantes, and armed robberies filled the daily headlines. New Yorkers were under siege. But Bratton's budget was frozen. Indeed, after three decades of mounting crime in New York City, many social scientists had concluded that it was impervious to police intervention. The citizens of New York City were crying out. A front-page headline in the *New York Post* had screamed: "Dave do something!"—a direct call to then mayor David Dinkins to get crime down fast.[1] With miserable pay, dangerous working conditions, long hours, and little hope of advancement in a tenure promotion system, morale among the NYPD's thirty-six thousand officers was at rock bottom—not to mention the debilitating effects of budget cuts, dilapidated equipment, and corruption.

In business terms, the NYPD was a cash-strapped organization with thirty-six thousand employees wedded to the status quo, unmotivated, and underpaid; a disgruntled customer base—New York City's citizens; and rapidly declining performance as measured by the increase in crime, fear, and disorder. Entrenched turf wars and politics topped off the cake. In short, leading the NYPD to execute a shift in strategy was a managerial nightmare far beyond the imaginations of most executives. The competition—the criminals—was strong and rising.

Yet in less than two years and without an increase in his budget, Bratton turned New York City into the safest large city in the United States. He broke out of the red ocean with a blue ocean policing strategy that revolutionized U.S. policing as it was then known. Between 1994 and 1996, the organization won as "profits" jumped: Felony crime fell 39 percent, murders 50 percent, and theft 35 percent. "Customers" won: Gallup polls reported that public confidence in the NYPD leaped from 37 percent to 73 percent. And employees won: Internal surveys showed job satisfaction in the NYPD reaching an all-time high. As one patrolman put it, "We would have marched to hell and back for that guy." Perhaps most impressively, the changes have outlasted its leader, implying a fundamental shift in the organizational culture and strategy of the NYPD. Even after Bratton's departure in 1996, crime rates have continued to fall.

Few corporate leaders face organizational hurdles as steep as Bratton did in executing a break from the status quo. And still fewer are able to orchestrate the type of performance leap that Bratton achieved under any organizational conditions, let alone those as stringent as he encountered. Even Jack Welch needed some ten years and tens of millions of dollars of restructuring and training to turn GE into a powerhouse.

Moreover, defying conventional wisdom, Bratton achieved these breakthrough results in record time with scarce resources while

FIGURE 7-1

The Four Organizational Hurdles to Strategy Execution

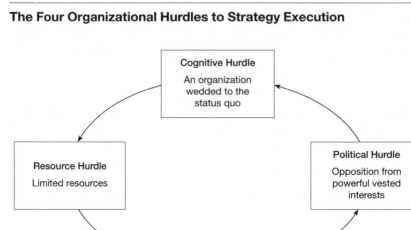

lifting employee morale, creating a win-win for all involved. Nor was this Bratton's first strategic reversal. It was his fifth, with each of the others also achieved despite his facing all four hurdles that managers consistently claim limit their ability to execute blue ocean strategy: the cognitive hurdle that blinds employees from seeing that radical change is necessary; the resource hurdle that is endemic in firms; the motivational hurdle that discourages and demoralizes staff; and the political hurdle of internal and external resistance to change (see figure 7-1).

The Pivotal Lever: Disproportionate Influence Factors

Tipping point leadership traces its roots to the field of epidemiology and the theory of tipping points.[2] It hinges on the insight that in any organization, fundamental changes can happen quickly when the beliefs and energies of a critical mass of people create an epidemic movement toward an idea. Key to unlocking an epidemic movement is concentration, not diffusion.

Tipping point leadership builds on the rarely exploited corporate reality that in every organization, there are *people, acts*, and *activities* that exercise a *disproportionate influence* on performance. Hence, contrary to conventional wisdom, mounting a massive challenge is not about putting forth an equally massive response where performance gains are achieved by proportional investments in time and resources. Rather, it is about conserving resources and cutting time by focusing on identifying and then leveraging the factors of disproportionate influence in an organization.

The key questions answered by tipping point leaders are as follows: What factors or acts exercise a disproportionately positive influence on breaking the status quo? On getting the maximum bang out of each buck of resources? On motivating key players to aggressively move forward with change? And on knocking down political roadblocks that often trip up even the best strategies? By single-mindedly focusing on points of disproportionate influence, tipping point leaders can topple the four hurdles that limit execution of blue ocean strategy. They can do this fast and at low cost.

Let us consider how you can leverage disproportionate influence factors to tip all four hurdles to move from thought to action in the execution of blue ocean strategy.

Break Through the Cognitive Hurdle

In many turnarounds and corporate transformations, the hardest battle is simply to make people aware of the need for a strategic shift and to agree on its causes. Most CEOs will try to make the case for change simply by pointing to the numbers and insisting that the company set and achieve better results: "There are only two performance alternatives: to make the performance targets or to beat them."

But as we all know, figures can be manipulated. Insisting on stretch goals encourages abuse in the budgetary process. This, in turn, creates hostility and suspicion between the various parts of an organization. Even when the numbers are not manipulated, they can mislead. Salespeople on commission, for example, are seldom sensitive to the costs of the sales they produce.

What's more, messages communicated through numbers seldom stick with people. The case for change feels abstract and removed from the sphere of the line managers, who are the very people the CEO needs to win over. Those whose units are doing well feel that the criticism is not directed at them; the problem is top management's. Meanwhile, managers of poorly performing units feel that they are being put on notice, and people who are worried about personal job security are more likely to scan the job market than to try to solve the company's problems.

Tipping point leadership does not rely on numbers to break through the organization's cognitive hurdle. To tip the cognitive hurdle fast, tipping point leaders such as Bratton zoom in on the act of disproportionate influence: making people see and experience harsh reality firsthand. Research in neuroscience and cognitive science shows that people remember and respond most effectively to what they see and experience: "Seeing is believing." In the realm of experience, positive stimuli reinforce behavior, whereas negative stimuli change attitudes and behavior. Simply put, if a child puts a finger in icing and tastes it, the better it tastes the more the child will taste it repetitively. No parental advice is needed to encourage that behavior. Conversely, after a child puts a finger on a burning stove, he or she will never do it again. After a negative experience, children will change their behavior of their own accord; again, no parental pestering is required.[3] On the other hand, experiences that don't involve touching, seeing, or feeling actual results, such as being presented with an abstract sheet of numbers, are shown to be non-impactful and easily forgotten.[4]

Tipping point leadership builds on this insight to inspire a fast change in mindset that is *internally driven of people's own accord.*

Instead of relying on numbers to tip the cognitive hurdle, they make people experience the need for change in two ways.

Ride the "Electric Sewer"

To break the status quo, employees must come face-to-face with the worst operational problems. Don't let top brass, middle brass, or any brass hypothesize about reality. Numbers are disputable and uninspiring, but coming face-to-face with poor performance is shocking and inescapable, but actionable. This direct experience exercises a disproportionate influence on tipping people's cognitive hurdle fast.

Consider this example. In the 1990s the New York subway system reeked of fear, so much so that it earned the epithet "electric sewer." Revenues were tumbling fast as citizens boycotted the system. But members of the New York City Transit Police department were in denial. Why? Only 3 percent of the city's major crimes happened on the subway. So no matter how much the public cried out, their cries fell on deaf ears. There was no perceived need to rethink police strategies.

Then Bratton was appointed chief, and in a matter of weeks he orchestrated a complete break from the status quo in the mindset of the city's police. How? Not by force, nor by arguing for numbers, but by making top brass and middle brass—starting with himself— ride the electric sewer day and night. Until Bratton came along, that had not been done.

Although the statistics may have told the police that the subway was safe, what they now saw was what every New Yorker faced every day: a subway system on the verge of anarchy. Gangs of youths patrolled the cars, people jumped turnstiles, and the riders faced graffiti, aggressive begging, and winos sprawled over benches. The police could no longer evade the ugly truth. No one could argue that current police strategies didn't require a substantial departure from the status quo—and fast.

Showing the worst reality to your superiors can also shift their mindset fast. A similar approach works to help sensitize superiors to a leader's needs fast. Yet few leaders exploit the power of this rapid wake-up call. Rather, they do the opposite. They try to garner support based on a numbers case that lacks urgency and emotional impetus. Or they try to put forth the most exemplary case of their operational excellence to garner support. Although these alternatives may work, neither leads to tipping superiors' cognitive hurdle as fast and stunningly as showing the worst.

When Bratton, for example, was running the police division of the Massachusetts Bay Transportation Authority (MBTA), the MBTA board decided to purchase small squad cars that would be cheaper to buy and to run. That went against Bratton's new policing strategy. Instead of fighting the decision, however, or arguing for a larger budget—something that would have taken months to reevaluate and probably would have been rejected in the end— Bratton invited the MBTA's general manager for a tour of his unit to see the district.

To let the general manager see the horror he was trying to rectify, Bratton picked him up in a small car just like the ones that were being ordered. He jammed the seats up front to let the manager feel how little legroom a six-foot cop would get, and then Bratton drove over every pothole he could. Bratton also put on his belt, cuffs, and gun for the trip so that the manager would see how little space there was for the tools of the police officer's trade. After two hours, the general manager wanted out. He told Bratton he didn't know how Bratton could stand being in such a cramped car for so long on his own, never mind having a criminal in the back seat. Bratton got the larger cars his new strategy demanded.

Meet with Disgruntled Customers

To tip the cognitive hurdle, not only must you get your managers out of the office to see operational horror, but also you must get them to listen to their most disgruntled customers firsthand. Don't rely on market surveys. To what extent does your top team actively observe the market firsthand and meet with your most disgruntled customers to hear their concerns? Do you ever wonder why sales don't match your confidence in your product? Simply put, there is no substitute for meeting and listening to dissatisfied customers directly.

In the late 1970s, Boston's Police District 4, which housed the Symphony Hall, Christian Science Mother Church, and other cultural institutions, was experiencing a serious surge in crime. The public was increasingly intimidated; residents were selling their homes and leaving, thereby pushing the community into a downward spiral. But even though the citizens were leaving the area in droves, the police force under Bratton's direction felt they were doing a fine job. The performance indicators they historically used to benchmark themselves against other police departments were tip-top: 911 response times were down, and felony crime arrests were up. To solve the paradox Bratton arranged a series of town hall meetings between his officers and the neighborhood residents.

It didn't take long to find the gap in perceptions. Although the police officers took great pride in short response times and their record in solving major crimes, these efforts went unnoticed and unappreciated by citizens; few felt endangered by large-scale crimes. What they felt victimized by and harassed by were the constant minor irritants: winos, panhandlers, prostitutes, and graffiti.

The town meetings led to a complete overhaul of police priorities to focus on the blue ocean strategy of "broken windows."[5] Crime went down, and the neighborhood felt safe again.

When you want to wake up your organization to the need for a strategic shift and a break from the status quo, do you make your case with numbers? Or do you get your managers, employees, and superiors (and yourself) face-to-face with your worst operational problems? Do you get your managers to meet the market and listen to disenchanted customers holler? Or do you outsource your eyes and send out market research questionnaires?

Jump the Resource Hurdle

After people in an organization accept the need for a strategic shift and more or less agree on the contours of the new strategy, most leaders are faced with the stark reality of limited resources. Do they have the money to spend on the necessary changes? At this point, most reformist CEOs do one of two things. Either they trim their ambitions and demoralize their work force all over again, or they fight for more resources from their bankers and shareholders, a process that can take time and divert attention from the underlying problems. That's not to say that this approach is not necessary or worthwhile, but acquiring more resources is often a long, politically charged process.

How do you get an organization to execute a strategic shift with fewer resources? Instead of focusing on getting more resources, tipping point leaders concentrate on multiplying the value of the resources they have. When it comes to scarce resources, there are three factors of disproportionate influence that executives can leverage to dramatically free resources, on the one hand, and multiply the value of resources, on the other. These are hot spots, cold spots, and horse trading.

Hot spots are activities that have low resource input but high potential performance gains. In contrast, *cold spots* are activities that have high resource input but low performance impact. In every organization, hot spots and cold spots typically abound. *Horse trading* involves trading your unit's excess resources in one area for another unit's excess resources to fill remaining resource gaps. By learning to use their current resources right, companies often find they can tip the resource hurdle outright.

What actions consume your greatest resources but have scant performance impact? Conversely, what activities have the greatest performance impact but are resource starved? When the questions are framed in this way, organizations rapidly gain insight into freeing up low-return resources and redirecting them to high-impact areas. In this way, both lower costs and higher value are simultaneously pursued and achieved.

Redistribute Resources to Your Hot Spots

At the New York Transit Police, Bratton's predecessors argued that to make the city's subways safe they had to have an officer ride every subway line and patrol every entrance and exit. To increase profits (lower crime) would mean increasing costs (police officers) in multiples that were not possible given the budget. The underlying logic was that increments in performance could be achieved only with proportional increments in resources—the same inherent logic guiding most companies' view of performance gains.

Bratton, however, achieved the sharpest drop in subway crime, fear, and disorder in Transit's history, not with more police officers but with police officers targeted at hot spots. His analysis revealed that although the subway system was a maze of lines and entrances and exits, the vast majority of crimes occurred at only a few stations and on a few lines. He also found that these hot spots were starved for police attention even though they exercised a disproportionate impact on crime performance, whereas lines and stations that almost never reported criminal activity were staffed equally. The solution was a complete refocusing of cops at subway hot spots to overwhelm the criminal element. And crime came tumbling down while the size of the police force remained constant.

Similarly, before Bratton's arrival at the NYPD the narcotics unit worked nine-to-five weekday-only shifts and made up less than 5 percent of the department's human resources. To search out resource hot spots, in one of his initial meetings with the NYPD's chiefs Bratton's deputy commissioner of crime strategy, Jack Maple, asked people around the table for their estimates of the percentage of crimes attributable to narcotics usage. Most said 50 percent, others 70 percent; the lowest estimate was 30 percent. On that basis, as Maple pointed out, it was hard to argue that a narcotics unit consisting of less than 5 percent of the NYPD force was not grossly understaffed. What's more, it turned out that the narcotics squad largely worked Monday to Friday, even though most drugs were sold over the weekend, when drug-related crimes persistently occurred. Why? That was the way it had always been; it was the unquestioned modus operandi.

When these facts were presented and the hot spot identified, Bratton's case for a major reallocation of staff and resources within the NYPD was quickly accepted. Accordingly, Bratton reallocated staff and resources on the hot spot, and drug crime plummeted.

Where did he get the resources to do this? He simultaneously assessed his organization's cold spots.

Redirect Resources from Your Cold Spots

Leaders need to free up resources by searching out cold spots. Again in the subway, Bratton found that one of the biggest cold spots was processing criminals in court. On average, it would take an officer sixteen hours to take someone downtown to process even the pettiest of crimes. This was time officers were not patrolling the subway and adding value.

Bratton changed all that. Instead of bringing criminals to the court, he brought processing centers to the criminals by using "bust buses"—roving old buses retrofitted into miniature police stations that were parked outside subway stations. Now instead of dragging a suspect down to the courthouse across town, a police officer needed only escort the suspect up to street level to the bus. This cut processing time from sixteen hours to just one, freeing more officers to patrol the subway and catch criminals.

Engage in Horse Trading

In addition to internally refocusing the resources a unit already controls, tipping point leaders skillfully trade resources they don't need for those of others that they do need. Consider again the case of Bratton. The chiefs of public sector organizations know that the size of their budgets and the number of people they control are often hotly debated because public sector resources are notoriously limited. This makes chiefs of public sector organizations unwilling to advertise excess resources, let alone release them for use by other parts of the larger organization, because that would risk a loss of control over those resources. One result is that over time, some organizations become well endowed with resources they don't need even while they are short of ones they do need.

On taking over as chief of the New York Transit Police in 1990, Bratton's general counsel and policy adviser, Dean Esserman (now police chief of Providence, Rhode Island), played a key horse trading role. Esserman discovered that the Transit unit, which was starved for office space, had been running a fleet of unmarked cars in excess of its needs. The New York Division of Parole, on the other hand, was short of cars but had excess office space. Esserman and Bratton offered the obvious trade, which was gratefully accepted by the parole officials. For their part, Transit unit officers were delighted to get the first floor of a prime downtown building. The deal stoked Bratton's credibility within the organization, something that later made it easier for him to introduce more fundamental changes. At the same time, it marked him to his political bosses as a man who could solve problems.

Figure 7-2 illustrates how radically Bratton refocused the Transit Police department's resources to break out of the red ocean and execute its blue ocean strategy. The vertical axis here shows the relative level of resource allocation, and the horizontal axis shows the various elements of strategy in which the investments were made. By deemphasizing or virtually eliminating some traditional features of transit police work while increasing emphasis on the others or creating new ones, Bratton achieved a dramatic shift in resource allocation.

Whereas the actions of eliminating and reducing cut the costs for the organization, raising certain elements or creating new ones required added investments. As you can see on the strategy canvas, however, the overall investment of resources remained more or less

FIGURE 7-2

The Strategy Canvas of Transit: How Bratton Refocused Resources

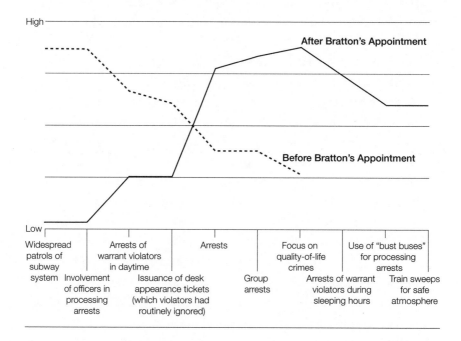

constant. At the same time, the value to citizens went way up. Eliminating the practice of widespread coverage of the subway system and replacing it with a targeted strategy on hot spots enabled the transit police to combat subway crimes more efficiently and effectively. Reducing the involvement of officers in processing arrests or cold spots and creating bust buses significantly raised the value of the police force by allowing officers to concentrate their time and attention on policing the subway. Raising the level of investment in combating quality-of-life crimes rather than big crimes refocused the police resources on crimes that presented constant dangers to citizens' daily lives. Through these moves, the New York Transit Police significantly enhanced the performance of its officers, who were now freed from administrative hassles and assigned clear duties as to what kinds of crimes they should focus on and where to combat them.

Are you allocating resources based on old assumptions, or do you seek out and concentrate resources on hot spots? Where are your hot spots? What activities have the greatest performance impact but are resource starved? Where are your cold spots? What activities are resource oversupplied but have scant performance impact? Do you have a horse trader, and what can you trade?

Jump the Motivational Hurdle

To reach your organization's tipping point and execute blue ocean strategy, you must alert employees to the need for a strategic shift and identify how it can be achieved with limited resources. For a new strategy to become a movement, people must not only recognize what needs to be done, but they must also act on that insight in a sustained and meaningful way.

How can you motivate the mass of employees fast and at low cost? When most business leaders want to break from the status quo and transform their organizations, they issue grand strategic visions and turn to massive top-down mobilization initiatives. They act on the assumption that to create massive reactions, proportionate massive actions are required. But this is often a cumbersome, expensive, and time-consuming process, given the wide variety of motivational needs in most large companies. And overarching strategic visions often inspire lip service instead of the intended action. It would be easier to turn an aircraft carrier around in a bathtub.

Or is there another way? Instead of diffusing change efforts widely, tipping point leaders follow a reverse course and seek massive concentration. They focus on three factors of disproportionate influence in motivating employees, what we call kingpins, fishbowl management, and atomization.

Zoom in on Kingpins

For strategic change to have real impact, employees at every level must move en masse. To trigger an epidemic movement of positive energy, however, you should not spread your efforts thin. Rather, you should concentrate your efforts on *kingpins*, the key influencers in the organization. These are people inside the organization who are natural leaders, who are well respected and persuasive, or who have an ability to unlock or block access to key resources. As with kingpins in bowling, when you hit them straight on, all the other pins come toppling down. This frees an organization from tackling everyone, and yet in the end everyone is touched and changed. And because in most organizations there are a relatively small number of key influencers, who tend to share common problems and concerns, it is relatively easy for the CEO to identify and motivate them.

At the NYPD, for example, Bratton zoomed in on the seventy-six precinct heads as his key influencers and kingpins. Why? Each precinct head directly controlled two hundred to four hundred police officers. Hence, galvanizing these seventy-six heads would have the natural ripple effect of touching and motivating the thirty-six-thousand-deep police force to embrace the new policing strategy.

Place Kingpins in a Fishbowl

At the heart of motivating the kingpins in a sustained and meaningful way is to shine a spotlight on their actions in a repeated and highly visible way. This is what we refer to as *fishbowl* management, where kingpins' actions and inaction are made as transparent to others as are fish in a bowl of water. By placing kingpins in a fishbowl in this way you greatly raise the stakes of inaction. Light is shined on who is lagging behind, and a fair stage is set for rapid change agents to shine. For fishbowl management to work it must be based on transparency, inclusion, and fair process.

At the NYPD, Bratton's fishbowl was a biweekly crime strategy review meeting known as Compstat that brought together the city's top brass to review the performance of all the seventy-six precinct commanders in executing its new strategy. Attendance was mandatory for all precinct commanders; three-star chiefs, deputy commissioners, and borough chiefs were also required to attend. Bratton himself was there as often as possible. As each precinct commander was questioned on decreases and increases in crime performance in front of peers and superiors based on the organization's new strategic directives, enormous computer-generated overhead maps and charts were shown, visually illustrating in inescapable terms the commander's performance in executing the new strategy. The commander was responsible for explaining the maps, describing how his or her officers were addressing the issues, and outlining why performance was going up or down. These inclusive meetings instantly made results and responsibilities clear and transparent for everyone.

As a result, an intense performance culture was created in weeks—forget about months, let alone years—because no kingpin wanted to be shamed in front of others, and they all wanted to shine in front of their peers and superiors. In the fishbowl, incompetent precinct commanders could no longer cover up their failings by blaming their precinct's results on the shortcomings of neighboring precincts, because their neighbors were in the room and could respond. Indeed, a picture of the precinct commander to be grilled at the crime strategy meetings was printed on the front page of the handout, emphasizing that the commander was responsible and accountable for that precinct's results.

By the same token, the fishbowl gave an opportunity for high achievers to gain recognition for work in their own precincts and in helping others. The meetings also provided an opportunity for policy leaders to compare notes on their experiences; before Bratton's arrival, precinct commanders seldom got together as a group. Over time, this style of fishbowl management filtered down the ranks, as the precinct commanders tried out their own versions of Bratton's meetings. With the spotlight shining brightly on their performance in strategy execution, the precinct commanders were highly motivated to get all the officers under their control marching to the new strategy.

For this to work, however, organizations must simultaneously make fair process the modus operandi. By *fair process* we mean engaging all the affected people in the process, explaining to them the basis of decisions and the reasons people will be promoted or sidestepped in the future, and setting clear expectations of what that means to employees' performance. At the NYPD's crime strategy review meetings, no one could argue that the playing field wasn't fair. The fishbowl was applied to all kingpins. There was clear transparency in the assessment of every commander's performance and how it would tie into advancement or demotion, and clear expectations were set in every meeting of what was expected in performance from everyone.

In this way, fair process signals to people that there is a level playing field and that leaders value employees' intellectual and emotional worth despite all the change that may be required. This greatly mitigates feelings of suspicion and doubt that are almost necessarily present in employees' minds when a company is trying to make a major strategic shift. The cushion of support provided by fair process, combined with the fishbowl emphasis on sheer performance, pushes people and supports them on the journey, demonstrating managers' intellectual and emotional respect for employees. (For a fuller discussion on fair process and its motivational implications, see chapter 8.)

Atomize to Get the Organization to Change Itself

The last disproportionate influence factor is atomization. *Atomization* relates to the framing of the strategic challenge—one of the most subtle and sensitive tasks of the tipping point leader. Unless people believe that the strategic challenge is attainable, the change is not likely to succeed. On the face of it, Bratton's goal in New York City was so ambitious as to be scarcely believable. Who could believe that anything an individual could do would turn such a huge city from being the most dangerous place in the country into the safest? And who would want to invest time and energy in chasing an impossible dream?

To make the challenge attainable, Bratton broke it into bite-size atoms that officers at different levels could relate to. As he put it, the challenge facing the NYPD was to make the streets of New York City safe "block by block, precinct by precinct, and borough by borough." Thus framed, the challenge was both all-encompassing and doable. For officers on the street, the challenge was to make their beat or block safe—no more. For the precinct commanders, the challenge was to make their precinct safe—no more. Borough heads also had a concrete goal within their capabilities: making their boroughs safe—no more. No one could say that what was being asked of them was too tough. Nor could they claim that achieving it was largely out of their hands—"It's beyond me." In this way, responsibility for executing Bratton's blue ocean strategy shifted from him to each of the NYPD's thirty-six thousand officers.

Do you indiscriminately try to motivate the masses? Or do you focus on key influencers, your kingpins? Do you put the spotlight on and manage kingpins in a fishbowl based on fair process? Or do you just demand high performance and cross your fingers until the next quarter numbers come out? Do you issue grand strategic visions? Or do you atomize the issue to make it actionable to all levels?

Knock Over the Political Hurdle

Youth and skill will win out every time over age and treachery. True or false? False. Even the best and brightest are regularly eaten alive by politics, intrigue, and plotting. Organizational politics is an inescapable reality of corporate and public life. Even if an organization has reached the tipping point of execution, there exist powerful vested interests that will resist the impending changes. (Also see our discussion on adoption hurdles in chapter 6.) The more likely change becomes, the more fiercely and vocally these negative influencers—both internal and external—will fight to protect their positions, and their resistance can seriously damage and even derail the strategy execution process.

To overcome these political forces, tipping point leaders focus on three disproportionate influence factors: leveraging angels, silencing devils, and getting a consigliere on their top management team. *Angels* are those who have the most to gain from the strategic shift. *Devils* are those who have the most to lose from it. And a *consigliere* is a politically adept but highly respected insider who knows in advance all the land mines, including who will fight you and who will support you.

Secure a Consigliere on Your Top Management Team

Most leaders concentrate on building a top management team having strong functional skills such as marketing, operations, and finance—and that is important. Tipping point leaders, however, also engage one role few other executives think to include: a consigliere. To that end, Bratton, for example, always ensured that he had a respected senior insider on his top team who knew the land mines he would face in implementing the new policing strategy. At NYPD, Bratton appointed John Timoney (now the police commissioner of Miami) as his number two. Timoney was a cop's cop, respected and feared for his dedication to the NYPD and for the more than sixty decorations and combat crosses he had received. Twenty years in the ranks had taught him not only who all the key players were but also how they played the political game. One of the first tasks Timoney did was to report to Bratton on the likely attitudes of the top staff to the NYPD's new policing strategy, identifying those who would fight or silently sabotage the new initiative. This led to a dramatic changing of the guard.

Leverage Your Angels and Silence Your Devils

To knock down the political hurdles, you should also ask yourself two sets of questions:

- Who are my devils? Who will fight me? Who will lose the most by the future blue ocean strategy?

- Who are my angels? Who will naturally align with me? Who will gain the most by the strategic shift?

Don't fight alone. Get the higher and wider voice to fight with you. Identify your detractors and supporters—forget the middle—and strive to create a win-win outcome for both. But move quickly. Isolate your detractors by building a broader coalition with your angels before a battle begins. In this way, you will discourage the war before it has a chance to start or gain steam.

One of the most serious threats to Bratton's new policing strategy came from New York City's courts. Believing that Bratton's new policing strategy of focusing on quality-of-life crimes would overwhelm the system with small crime cases such as prostitution and public drunkenness, the courts opposed the strategic shift. To overcome this opposition, Bratton clearly illustrated to his supporters, including the mayor, district attorneys, and jail managers, that the court system could indeed handle the added quality-of-life crimes and that focusing on them would, in the long term, actually reduce their caseload. The mayor decided to intervene.

Then Bratton's coalition, led by the mayor, went on the offensive in the press with a clear and simple message: If the courts did not pull their weight, the city's crime rate would not go down. Bratton's alliance with the mayor's office and the city's leading newspaper successfully isolated the courts. They could hardly be seen to publicly oppose an initiative that would not only make New York a more attractive place to live but would also ultimately reduce the number of cases brought before them. With the mayor speaking aggressively in the press of the need to pursue quality-of-life crimes and the city's most respected—and liberal—newspaper giving credence to the new police strategy, the costs of fighting Bratton's strategy were daunting. Bratton had won the battle: The courts would comply. He also won the war: Crime rates did indeed come down.

Key to winning over your detractors or devils is knowing all their likely angles of attack and building up counterarguments backed by irrefutable facts and reason. For example, when the NYPD's precinct commanders were first requested to compile detailed crime data and maps, they balked at the idea, arguing that it would take too much time. Anticipating this reaction, Bratton had already done a test run of the operation to see how long it would take: no more than eighteen minutes a day, which worked out, as he told the commanders, to less than 1 percent of their average workload. Armed with irrefutable information, he was able to tip the political hurdle and win the battle before it even began.

Do you have a consigliere—a highly respected insider—in your top management team, or only a CFO and other functional head heads? Do you know who will fight you and who will align with the new strategy? Have you built coalitions with natural allies to encircle dissidents? Do you have your consigliere remove the biggest land mines so that you don't have to focus on changing those who cannot and will not change?

Challenging Conventional Wisdom

As shown in figure 7-3, the conventional theory of organizational change rests on transforming the mass. So change efforts are focused on moving the mass, requiring steep resources and long time frames—luxuries few executives can afford. Tipping point leadership, by contrast, takes a reverse course. To change the mass it focuses on transforming the extremes: the people, acts, and activities that exercise a disproportionate influence on performance. By transforming the extremes, tipping point leaders are able to change the core fast and at low cost to execute their new strategy.

FIGURE 7-3

Conventional Wisdom Versus Tipping Point Leadership

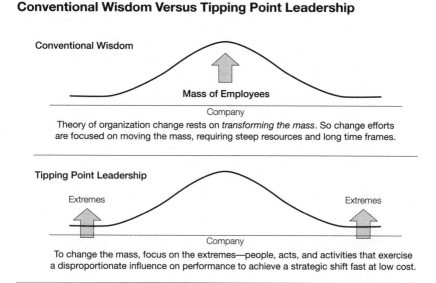

Conventional Wisdom

Mass of Employees

Company

Theory of organization change rests on *transforming the mass*. So change efforts are focused on moving the mass, requiring steep resources and long time frames.

Tipping Point Leadership

Extremes   Extremes

Company

To change the mass, focus on the extremes—people, acts, and activities that exercise a disproportionate influence on performance to achieve a strategic shift fast at low cost.

It is never easy to execute a strategic shift, and doing it fast with limited resources is even more difficult. Yet our research suggests that it can be achieved by leveraging tipping point leadership. By consciously addressing the hurdles to strategy execution and focusing on factors of disproportionate influence, you too can knock them over to actualize a strategic shift. Don't follow conventional wisdom. Not every challenge requires a proportionate action. Focus on acts of disproportionate influence. This is a critical leadership component for making blue ocean strategy happen. It aligns employees' actions with the new strategy.

The next chapter drills down one level further. It addresses the challenge of aligning people's minds and hearts with the new strategy by building a culture of trust, commitment, and voluntary cooperation in its execution, as well as support for the leader. Addressing this challenge spells the difference between forced execution and voluntary execution driven by people's free will.

CHAPTER 8

Build Execution into Strategy

A COMPANY IS NOT ONLY TOP MANAGEMENT, nor is it only middle management. A company is everyone from the top to the front lines. And it is only when all the members of an organization are aligned around a strategy and support it, for better or for worse, that a company stands apart as a great and consistent executor. Overcoming the organizational hurdles to strategy execution is an important step toward that end. It removes the roadblocks that can put a halt to even the best of strategies.

But in the end, a company needs to invoke the most fundamental base of action: the attitudes and behavior of its people deep in the organization. You must create a culture of trust and commitment that motivates people to execute the agreed strategy—not to the letter, but to the spirit. People's minds and hearts must align with the new strategy so that at the level of the individual, people embrace it of their own accord and willingly go beyond compulsory execution to voluntary cooperation in carrying it out.

Where blue ocean strategy is concerned, this challenge is heightened. Trepidation builds as people are required to step out of their comfort zones and change how they have worked in the past. They wonder, What are the real reasons for this change? Is top management honest when it speaks of building future growth through a change in strategic course? Or are they trying to make us redundant and work us out of our jobs?

The more removed people are from the top and the less they have been involved in the creation of the strategy, the more this trepidation builds. On the front line, at the very level at which a strategy must be executed day in and day out, people can resent having a strategy thrust upon them with little regard for what they think and feel. Just when you think you have done everything right, things can suddenly go very wrong in your front line.

This brings us to the sixth principle of blue ocean strategy: To build people's trust and commitment deep in the ranks and inspire their voluntary cooperation, companies need to build execution into strategy from the start. That principle allows companies to minimize the management risk of distrust, noncooperation, and even sabotage. This management risk is relevant to strategy execution in both red and blue oceans, but it is greater for blue ocean strategy because its execution often requires significant change. Hence, minimizing such risk is essential as companies execute blue ocean strategy. Companies must reach beyond the usual suspects of carrots and sticks. They must reach to fair process in the making and executing of strategy.

Our research shows that fair process is a key variable that distinguishes successful blue ocean strategic moves from those that failed. The presence or absence of fair process can make or break a company's best execution efforts.

Poor Process Can Ruin Strategy Execution

Consider the experience of a global leader in supplying water-based liquid coolants for metalworking industries. We'll call this organization Lubber. Because of the many processing parameters in metal-based manufacturing, there are several hundred complex types of coolants to choose from. Choosing the right coolant is a delicate process. Products must first be tested on production machines before purchasing, and the decision often rests on fuzzy logic. The result is machine downtime and sampling costs, and these are expensive for customers and Lubber alike.

To offer customers a leap in value, Lubber devised a strategy to eliminate the complexity and costs of the trial phase. Using artificial intelligence, it developed an expert system that cut the failure rate in selecting coolants to less than 10 percent from an industry average of 50 percent. The system also reduced machine downtime, eased coolant management, and raised the overall quality of work pieces produced. As for Lubber, the sales process was dramatically simplified, giving sales representatives more time to gain new sales and dropping the costs per sale.

This win-win value innovation strategic move, however, was doomed from the start. It wasn't that the strategy was not good or that the expert system did not work; it worked exceptionally well. The strategy was doomed because the sales force fought it.

Having not been engaged in the strategy-making process nor apprised of the rationale for the strategic shift, sales reps saw the expert system in a light no one on the design team or management team had ever imagined. To them, it was a direct threat to what they saw as their most valuable contribution—tinkering in the trial phase to find the right water-based coolant from the long list of possible candidates. All the wonderful benefits—having a way to avoid the hassle-filled part of their job, having more time to pull in more sales, and winning more contracts by standing out in the industry—went unappreciated.

With the sales force feeling threatened and often working against the expert system by expressing doubts about its effectiveness to customers, sales did not take off. After cursing its hubris and learning the hard way the importance of dealing with managerial risk up front based on the proper process, management was forced to pull the expert system from the market and work on rebuilding trust with its sales representatives.

The Power of Fair Process

What, then, is fair process? And how does it allow companies to build execution into strategy? The theme of fairness or justice has preoccupied writers and philosophers throughout the ages. But the direct theoretical origin of fair process traces back to two social scientists: John W. Thibaut and Laurens Walker. In the mid-1970s, they combined their interest in the psychology of justice with the study of process, creating the term *procedural justice*.[1] Focusing their attention on legal settings, they sought to understand what makes people trust a legal system so that they will comply with laws without being coerced. Their research established that people

FIGURE 8-1

How Fair Process Affects People's Attitudes and Behavior

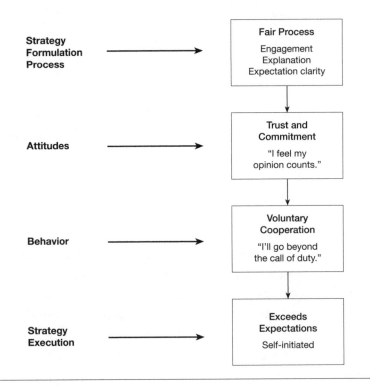

care as much about the justice of the process through which an outcome is produced as they do about the outcome itself. People's satisfaction with the outcome and their commitment to it rose when procedural justice was exercised.[2]

Fair process is our managerial expression of procedural justice theory. As in legal settings, fair process builds execution into strategy by creating people's buy-in up front. When fair process is exercised in the strategy-making process, people trust that a level playing field exists. This inspires them to cooperate voluntarily in executing the resulting strategic decisions.

Voluntary cooperation is more than mechanical execution, where people do only what it takes to get by. It involves going beyond the call of duty, wherein individuals exert energy and initiative to the best of their abilities—even subordinating personal self-interest— to execute resulting strategies.[3] Figure 8-1 presents the causal flow we observed among fair process, attitudes, and behavior.

The Three E Principles of Fair Process

There are three mutually reinforcing elements that define fair process: engagement, explanation, and clarity of expectation. Whether people are senior executives or shop floor employees, they all look to these elements. We call them the *three E principles of fair process*.

Engagement means involving individuals in the strategic decisions that affect them by asking for their input and allowing them to refute the merits of one another's ideas and assumptions. Engagement communicates management's respect for individuals and their ideas. Encouraging refutation sharpens everyone's thinking and builds better collective wisdom. Engagement results in better strategic decisions by management and greater commitment from all involved to execute those decisions.

Explanation means that everyone involved and affected should understand why final strategic decisions are made as they are. An explanation of the thinking that underlies decisions makes people confident that managers have considered their opinions and have made decisions impartially in the overall interests of the company. An explanation allows employees to trust managers' intentions even if their own ideas have been rejected. It also serves as a powerful feedback loop that enhances learning.

Expectation clarity requires that after a strategy is set, managers state clearly the new rules of the game. Although the expectations may be demanding, employees should know up front what standards they will be judged by and the penalties for failure. What are the goals of the new strategy? What are the new targets and milestones? Who is responsible for what? To achieve fair process, it matters less what the new goals, expectations, and responsibilities are and more that they are clearly understood. When people clearly understand what is expected of them, political jockeying and favoritism are minimized, and people can focus on executing the strategy rapidly.

Taken together, these three criteria *collectively* lead to judgments of fair process. This is important, because any subset of the three does not create judgments of fair process.

A Tale of Two Plants

How do the three E principles of fair process work to affect strategy execution deep in an organization? Consider the experience of an elevator systems manufacturer we'll call Elco. In the late 1980s, sales in the elevator industry declined. Excess office space left some large U.S. cities with vacancy rates as high as 20 percent.

With domestic demand falling, Elco set out to offer buyers a leap in value while lowering its costs to stimulate new demand and break from the competition. In its quest to create and execute a blue ocean strategy, the company realized that it needed to replace its batch-manufacturing system with a cellular approach that would allow self-directed teams to achieve superior performance. The management team was in agreement and ready to go. To execute this key element of its strategy, the team adopted what looked like the fastest and smartest way to move forward.

It would first install the new system at Elco's Chester plant and then roll it out to its second plant, High Park. The logic was simple. The Chester plant had exemplary employee relations, so much so that the workers had decertified their own union. Management was certain it could count on employee cooperation to execute the strategic shift in manufacturing. In the company's words, "They were the ideal work force." Next, Elco would roll out the process to its plant in High Park, where a strong union was expected to resist that, or any other, change. Management was counting on having achieved a degree of momentum for execution at Chester that it hoped would have positive spillover effects on High Park.

The theory was good. In practice, however, things took an unpredicted turn. The introduction of the new manufacturing process at the Chester plant quickly led to disorder and rebellion. Within a few months, both cost and quality performance were in free fall. Employees were talking about bringing back the union. Having lost control, the despairing plant manager called Elco's industrial psychologist for help.

In contrast, the High Park plant, despite its reputation for resistance, had accepted the strategic shift in the manufacturing process. Every day, the High Park manager waited for the anticipated meltdown, but it never came. Even when people didn't like the decisions, they felt they had been treated fairly, and so they willingly participated in the rapid execution of the new manufacturing process, a pivotal component of the company's new strategy.

A closer look at the way the strategic shift was made at the two plants reveals the reasons behind this apparent anomaly. At the Chester plant, Elco managers violated all three of the basic principles of fair process. First, they failed to engage employees in the strategic decisions that directly affected them. Lacking expertise in cellular manufacturing, Elco brought in a consulting firm to design a master plan for the conversion. The consultants were briefed to work quickly and with minimal disturbance to employees so that fast, painless implementation could be achieved. The consultants followed the instructions. When Chester employees arrived at work they discovered strangers at the plant who not only dressed differently—wearing dark suits, white shirts, and ties—but also spoke in low tones to one another. To minimize disturbance, they didn't interact with employees. Instead they quietly hovered behind people's backs, taking notes and drawing diagrams. The rumor circulated that after employees went home in the afternoon, these same people would swarm across the plant floor, snoop around people's workstations, and have heated discussions.

During this period, the plant manager was increasingly absent. He was spending more time at Elco's head office in meetings with the consultants—sessions deliberately scheduled away from the plant so as not to distract the employees. But the plant manager's absence produced the opposite effect. As people grew anxious, wondering why the captain of their ship seemed to be deserting them, the rumor mill moved into high gear. Everyone became convinced that the consultants would downsize the plant. They were sure they were about to lose their jobs. The fact that the plant manager was always gone without any explanation—obviously, he was avoiding them—could only mean that management was, they thought, "trying to put one over on us." Trust and commitment at the Chester plant deteriorated quickly.

Soon, people were bringing in newspaper clippings about other plants around the country that had been shut down with the help of consultants. Employees saw themselves as imminent victims of management's hidden intention to downsize and work people out of their jobs. In fact, Elco managers had no intention of closing the plant. They wanted to cut waste, freeing people to produce higher-quality elevators faster at lower cost to leapfrog the competition. But plant employees could not have known that.

Managers at Chester also didn't explain why strategic decisions were being made the way they were and what those decisions meant to employees' careers and work methods. Management unveiled the master plan for change in a thirty-minute session with employees.

The audience heard that their time-honored way of working would be abolished and replaced by something called "cellular manufacturing." No one explained why the strategic shift was needed, how the company needed to break away from the competition to stimulate new demand, and why the shift in the manufacturing process was a key element of that strategy. Employees sat in stunned silence, with no understanding of the rationale behind the change. The managers mistook this for acceptance, forgetting how long it had taken them over the preceding few months to get comfortable with the idea of shifting to cellular manufacturing to execute the new strategy.

Master plan in hand, management quickly began rearranging the plant. When employees asked what the new layout aimed to achieve, the response was "efficiency gains." The managers didn't have time to explain why efficiency had to be improved and didn't want to worry employees. But lacking an intellectual understanding of what was happening to them, some employees began feeling sick as they came to work.

Managers also neglected to make clear what would be expected of employees under the new manufacturing process. They informed employees that they would no longer be judged on individual performance but rather on the performance of the cell. They said that faster or more experienced employees would have to pick up the slack for slower or less experienced colleagues. But they didn't elaborate. How the new cellular system was supposed to work, managers didn't make clear.

Violations of the principles of fair process undermined employees' trust in the strategic shift and in management. In fact, the new cell design offered tremendous benefits to employees—for example, making vacations easier to schedule and giving them the opportunity to broaden their skills and engage in a greater variety of work. Yet employees could see only its negative side. They began taking out their fear and anger on one another. Fights erupted on the plant floor as employees refused to help those they called "lazy people who can't finish their own jobs" or interpreted offers of help as meddling, responding with, "This is my job. You keep to your own workstation."

Chester's model work force was falling apart. For the first time in the plant manager's career, employees refused to do as they were asked, turning down assignments "even if you fire me." They felt they could no longer trust the once popular plant manager, so they began to go around him, taking their complaints directly to his boss at the head office. In the absence of fair process, the Chester plant's employees rejected the transformation and refused to play their role in executing the new strategy.

In contrast, management at the High Park plant abided by all three principles of fair process when introducing the strategic shift. When the consultants came to the plant, the plant manager introduced them to all employees. Management engaged employees by holding a series of plantwide meetings, where corporate executives openly discussed the declining business conditions and the company's need for a change in strategic course to break from the competition and simultaneously achieve higher value at lower cost. They explained that they had visited other companies' plants and had seen the productivity improvements that cellular manufacturing could bring. They explained how this would be a pivotal determinant of the company's ability to achieve its new strategy. They announced a proaction-time policy to calm employees' justifiable fears of layoffs. As old performance measures were discarded, managers worked with employees to develop new ones and to establish each cell team's new responsibilities. Goals and expectations were made clear to employees.

By practicing the three principles of fair process *in tandem*, management won the understanding and support of High Park employees. The employees spoke of their plant manager with admiration, and they commiserated with the difficulties Elco's managers had in executing the new strategy and making the changeover to cellular manufacturing. They concluded that it had been a necessary, worthwhile, and positive experience.

Elco's managers still regard this experience as one of the most painful in their careers. They learned that people in the front line care as much about the proper process as those at the top. By violating fair process in making and rolling out strategies, managers can turn their best employees into their worst, earning their distrust of and resistance to the very strategy they depend on them to execute. But if managers practice fair process, the worst employees can turn into the best and can execute even difficult strategic shifts with their willing commitment while building their trust.

Why Does Fair Process Matter?

Why is fair process important in shaping people's attitudes and behavior? Specifically, why does the observance or violation of fair process in strategy making have the power to make or break a strategy's execution? It all comes down to intellectual and emotional recognition.

Emotionally, individuals seek recognition of their value, not as "labor," "personnel," or "human resources" but as human beings who are treated with full respect and dignity and appreciated for their individual worth regardless of hierarchical level. Intellectually, individuals seek recognition that their ideas are sought after and given thoughtful reflection, and that others think enough of their intelligence to explain their thinking to them. Such frequently cited expressions in our interviews as "that goes for everyone I know" or "every person wants to feel" and constant references to "people" and "human beings" reinforce the point that managers must see the nearly universal value of the intellectual and emotional recognition that fair process conveys.

Intellectual and Emotional Recognition Theory

Using fair process in strategy making is strongly linked to both intellectual and emotional recognition. It proves through action that there is an eagerness to trust and cherish the individual as well as a deep-seated confidence in the individual's knowledge, talents, and expertise.

When individuals feel recognized for their intellectual worth, they are willing to share their knowledge; in fact, they feel inspired to impress and confirm the expectation of their intellectual value, suggesting active ideas and knowledge sharing. Similarly, when individuals are treated with emotional recognition, they feel emotionally tied to the strategy and inspired to give their all. Indeed, in Frederick Herzberg's classic study on motivation, recognition was found to inspire strong intrinsic motivation, causing people to go beyond the call of duty and engage in voluntary cooperation.[4] Hence, to the extent that fair process judgments convey intellectual and emotional recognition, people will better apply their knowledge and expertise, as well as their voluntary efforts to cooperate for the organization's success in executing strategy.

However, there is a flip side to this that is deserving of equal, if not more, attention: the violation of fair process and, with it, the violation of recognizing individuals' intellectual and emotional worth. The observed pattern of thought and behavior can be summarized as follows. If individuals are not treated as though their knowledge is valued, they will feel intellectual indignation and will not share their ideas and expertise; rather, they will hoard their best thinking and creative ideas, preventing new insights from seeing the light of day. What's more, they will reject others' intellectual worth as well. It's as if they were saying, "You don't value my ideas. So I don't value your ideas, nor do I trust in or care about the strategic decisions you've reached."

Similarly, to the extent that people's emotional worth is not recognized, they will feel angry and will not invest their energy in their actions; rather, they will drag their feet and apply counterefforts, including sabotage, as in the case of Elco's Chester plant. This often leads employees to push for rolling back strategies that have been imposed unfairly, even when the strategies themselves were good ones—critical to the company's success or beneficial to

FIGURE 8-2

The Execution Consequences of the Presence and Absence of Fair Process in Strategy Making

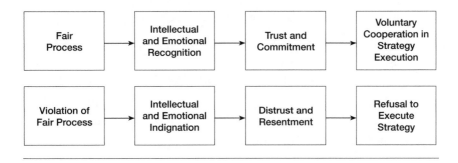

employees and managers themselves. Lacking trust in the strategy-making process, people lack trust in the resulting strategies. Such is the emotional power that fair process can provoke. Figure 8-2 shows the observed causal pattern.

Fair Process and Blue Ocean Strategy

Commitment, trust, and voluntary cooperation are not merely attitudes or behaviors. They are intangible capital. When people have trust, they have heightened confidence in one another's intentions and actions. When they have commitment, they are even willing to override personal self-interest in the interests of the company.

If you ask any company that has created and successfully executed a blue ocean strategy, managers will be quick to rattle off how important this intangible capital is to their success. Similarly, managers from companies that have failed in executing blue ocean strategies will point out that the lack of this capital contributed to their failure. These companies were not able to orchestrate strategic shifts because they lacked people's trust and commitment. Commitment, trust, and voluntary cooperation allow companies to stand apart in the speed, quality, and consistency of their execution and to implement strategic shifts fast at low cost.

The question companies wrestle with is how to create trust, commitment, and voluntary cooperation deep in the organization. You don't do it by separating strategy formulation from execution. Although this disconnect may be a hallmark of most companies' practice, it is also a hallmark of slow and questionable implementation, and mechanical follow-through at best. Of course, traditional incentives of power and money—carrots and sticks—help. But they fall short of inspiring human behavior that goes beyond outcome-driven self-interest. Where behavior cannot be monitored with certainty, there is still plenty of room for foot-dragging and sabotage.

The exercise of fair process gets around this dilemma. By organizing the strategy formulation process around the principles of fair process, you can build execution into strategy making from the start. With fair process, people tend to be committed to support the resulting strategy even when it is viewed as not favorable or at odds with their perception of what is strategically correct for their unit. People realize that compromises and sacrifices are necessary in building a strong company. They accept the need for short-term personal sacrifices in order to advance the long-term interests of the corporation. This acceptance is conditional, however, on the presence of fair process. Whatever the context in which a company's blue ocean strategy is executed—be it working with a joint venture partner to outsource component manufacturing, reorienting the sales force, transforming the manufacturing process, relocating a company's call center from the United States to India—we have consistently observed this dynamic at work.

CHAPTER 9

Conclusion: The Sustainability and Renewal of Blue Ocean Strategy

CREATING BLUE OCEANS is not a static achievement but a dynamic process. Once a company creates a blue ocean and its powerful performance consequences are known, sooner or later imitators appear on the horizon. The question is, How soon or late will they come? Put differently, how easy or difficult is blue ocean strategy to imitate?

As the company and its early imitators succeed and expand the blue ocean, more companies eventually jump in. This raises a related question: When should a company reach out to create another blue ocean? In this concluding chapter, we address the issues of the sustainability and renewal of blue ocean strategy.

Barriers to Imitation

A blue ocean strategy brings with it considerable barriers to imitation. Some of these are operational, and others are cognitive. More often than not, a blue ocean strategy will go without credible challenges for ten to fifteen years, as was the case with Cirque du Soleil, Southwest Airlines, Federal Express, The Home Depot, Bloomberg, and CNN, for starters. This sustainability can be traced to the following imitation barriers rooted in blue ocean strategy:

- A value innovation move does not make sense based on conventional strategic logic. When CNN was introduced, for example, NBC, CBS, and ABC ridiculed the idea of twenty-four-hour, seven-day, real-time news without star broadcasters. CNN was referred to as Chicken Noodle News by the industry. Ridicule does not inspire rapid imitation.

- Brand image conflict prevents companies from imitating a blue ocean strategy. The blue ocean strategy of The Body Shop, for example—which shunned beautiful models, promises of eternal beauty and youth, and expensive packaging— left major cosmetic houses the world over actionless for years because imitation would signal an invalidation of their current business models.

- Natural monopoly blocks imitation when the size of a market cannot support another player. For example, the Belgian cinema company Kinepolis created the first megaplex in Europe in the city of Brussels and has not been imitated in more than fifteen years despite its enormous success. The reason is that the size of Brussels could not support a second megaplex, which would cause both Kinepolis and its imitator to suffer.

- Patents or legal permits block imitation.

- The high volume generated by a value innovation leads to rapid cost advantages, placing potential imitators at an ongoing cost disadvantage. The huge economies of scale in purchasing enjoyed by Wal-Mart, for example, have significantly discouraged other companies from imitating its blue ocean strategy.

- Network externalities also block companies from easily and credibly imitating a blue ocean strategy, much as eBay enjoys in the online auction market. In short, the more customers eBay has online, the more attractive the auction site becomes for both sellers and buyers of wares, creating scant incentive for buyers to switch to a potential imitator.

- Because imitation often requires companies to make substantial changes to their existing business practices, politics often kick in, delaying for years a company's commitment to imitate a blue ocean strategy. When Southwest Airlines, for example, created a service that offered the speed of air travel with the cost and flexibility of driving, imitating this blue ocean strategy would have meant major revisions in routing planes, retraining staff, and changing marketing and pricing, not to mention culture—significant changes that the politics of few companies can bear in the short term.

- When a company offers a leap in value, it rapidly earns brand buzz and a loyal following in the marketplace. Even large advertising budgets by an aggressive imitator rarely have the strength to overtake the brand buzz earned by the value innovator. Microsoft, for example, has been trying for years to dislodge Intuit's value innovation, Quicken. More than ten years out, despite all its efforts and investment, it has not been able to do so.

Figure 9-1 provides a snapshot of these barriers to imitation. As the figure shows, the barriers are high. This is why we have seldom observed rapid imitation of blue ocean strategy. In addition, blue ocean strategy is a systems approach that requires not only getting each strategic element right but also aligning them in an integral system to deliver value innovation. Imitating such a system is not an easy feat.

FIGURE 9-1

Imitation Barriers to Blue Ocean Strategy

- Value innovation does not make sense to a company's conventional logic.
- Blue ocean strategy may conflict with other companies' brand image.
- Natural monopoly: The market often cannot support a second player.
- Patents or legal permits block imitation.
- High volume leads to rapid cost advantage for the value innovator, discouraging followers from entering the market.
- Network externalities discourage imitation.
- Imitation often requires significant political, operational, and cultural changes.
- Companies that value-innovate earn brand buzz and a loyal customer following that tends to shun imitators.

When to Value-Innovate Again

Eventually, however, almost every blue ocean strategy will be imitated. As imitators try to grab a share of your blue ocean, you typically launch offenses to defend your hard-earned customer base. But imitators often persist. Obsessed with hanging on to market share, you may fall into the trap of competing, racing to beat the new competition. Over time, the competition, and not the buyer, may come to occupy the center of your strategic thought and actions. If you stay on this course, the basic shape of your value curve will begin to converge with those of the competition.

To avoid the trap of competing, you need to monitor value curves on the strategy canvas. Monitoring value curves signals when to value-innovate and when not to. It alerts you to reach out for another blue ocean when your value curve begins to converge with those of the competition.

It also keeps you from pursuing another blue ocean when there is still a huge profit stream to be collected from your current offering. When the company's value curve still has focus, divergence, and a compelling tagline, you should resist the temptation to value-innovate again and instead should focus on lengthening, widening, and deepening your rent stream through operational improvements and geographical expansion to achieve maximum economies of scale and market coverage. You should swim as far as possible in the blue ocean, making yourself a moving target, distancing yourself from your early imitators, and discouraging them in the process. The aim here is to dominate the blue ocean over your imitators for as long as possible.

As rivalry intensifies and total supply exceeds demand, bloody competition commences and the ocean will turn red. As competitors' value curves converge toward yours, you should begin reaching out for another value innovation to create a new blue ocean. Hence, by charting your value curve on the strategy canvas and intermittently replotting your competitors' value curves versus your own, you will be able to visually see the degree of imitation, and hence of value curve convergence and the extent to which your blue ocean is turning red.

The Body Shop, for example, dominated the blue ocean it had created for more than a decade. The company, however, is now in the middle of a bloody red ocean, with declining performance. It did not reach out for another value innovation when competitors' value curves converged with its own. Similarly, [yellow tail] is swimming in the clear blue waters of new market space. It has made the competition irrelevant and is enjoying strong, profitable growth as a result. However, the test of Casella Wines' long-run profitable growth will be its ability to value-innovate again when imitators compete both aggressively and credibly with converging value curves.

The six principles of blue ocean strategy proposed in this book should serve as essential pointers for every company thinking about its future strategy if it aspires to lead the increasingly overcrowded business world. This is not to suggest that companies will suddenly stop competing or that the competition will suddenly come to a halt. On the contrary, the competition will be more present and will remain a critical factor of the market reality. What we suggest is that to obtain high performance in this overcrowded market, companies should go beyond competing for share to creating blue oceans.

Because blue and red oceans have always coexisted however, practical reality demands that companies succeed in both oceans and master the strategies for both. But because companies already understand how to compete in red oceans, what they need to learn is how to make the competition irrelevant. This book aims to help balance the scales so that formulating and executing blue ocean strategy can become as systematic and actionable as competing in the red oceans of known market space.

~~~~~~~~~~

A Sketch of the Historical Pattern of Blue Ocean Creation

AT THE RISK OF OVERSIMPLIFICATION, here we present a snapshot overview of the history of three American industries—automobiles, computers, and movie theaters—from the perspective of major product and service offerings that opened new market space and generated significant new demand. This review intends to be neither comprehensive in its coverage nor exhaustive in its content. Its aim is limited to identifying the common strategic elements across key blue ocean offerings. U.S. industries are chosen here because they represent the largest and least regulated free market during our study period.

Although the review is only a sketch of the historical pattern of blue ocean creation, several patterns stand out across these three representative industries.

- There is no permanently excellent industry. The attractiveness of all industries rose and fell over the study period.

- There are no permanently excellent companies. Companies, like industries, rose and fell over time. These first two findings both confirm and add further evidence that permanently excellent companies and industries do not exist.

- A key determinant of whether an industry or a company was on a rising trajectory of strong, profitable growth was the strategic move of blue ocean creation. The creation of blue oceans was a key catalyst in setting an industry on an upward growth and profit trajectory. It was also a pivotal determinant driving a company's rise in profitable growth, as well as its fall when another company gained the lead and created a new blue ocean.

- Blue oceans were created by both industry incumbents and new entrants, challenging the lore that start-ups have natural advantages over established companies in creating new market space. Moreover, the blue oceans created by incumbents were usually within their core businesses. In fact, most blue oceans are created from within, not beyond, red oceans of existing boundaries. Issues of perceived cannibalization or creative destruction for established companies proved to be exaggerated.[1] Blue oceans created profitable growth for every company launching them, start-ups and incumbents alike.

- The creation of blue oceans was not about technology innovation per se. Sometimes leading edge technology was present, but often it was not a defining feature of blue oceans. This was true even when the industry under examination was technology intensive, such as computers. Rather, the key defining feature of blue oceans was value innovation—innovation that was linked to what buyers value.

- The creation of blue oceans did more than contribute to strong, profitable growth; this strategic move exercised a strong, positive effect on establishing a company's standing brand name in buyers' minds.

Let's now turn to these three representative industries to let the history of blue ocean creation speak for itself. Here we begin with the auto industry, a central form of transportation in the developed world.

The Automobile Industry

The U.S. auto industry dates back to 1893, when the Duryea brothers launched the first one-cylinder auto in the United States. At the time, the horse and buggy was the primary means of U.S. transportation. Soon after the auto's U.S. debut, there were hundreds of auto manufacturers building custom-made automobiles in the country.

The autos of the time were a luxurious novelty. One model even offered electric curlers in the back seat for on-the-go primping. They were unreliable and expensive, costing around $1,500, twice the average annual family income. And they were enormously unpopular. Anticar activists tore up roads, ringed parked cars with barbed wire, and organized boycotts of car-driving businessmen and politicians. Public resentment of the automobile was so great that even future president Woodrow Wilson weighed in, saying, "Nothing has spread socialistic feeling more than the automobile . . . a picture of the arrogance of wealth."[2] *Literary Digest* suggested, "The ordinary 'horseless carriage' is at present a luxury for the wealthy; and although its price will probably fall in the future, it will never, of course, come into as common use as the bicycle."[3]

The industry, in short, was small and unattractive. Henry Ford, however, didn't believe it had to be this way.

The Model T

In 1908, while America's five hundred automakers built custom-made novelty automobiles, Henry Ford introduced the Model T. He called it the car "for the great multitude, constructed of the best materials." Although it came in only one color (black) and one model, the Model T was reliable, durable, and easy to fix. And it was priced so that the majority of Americans could afford one. In

1908 the first Model T cost $850, half the price of existing automobiles. In 1909 it dropped to $609, and by 1924 it was down to $290.[4] In comparison, the price of a horse-driven carriage, the car's closest alternative at the time, was around $400. A 1909 sales brochure proclaimed, "Watch the Ford Go By, High Priced Quality in a Low Priced Car."

Ford's success was underpinned by a profitable business model. By keeping the cars highly standardized and offering limited options and interchangeable parts, Ford's revolutionary assembly line replaced skilled craftsmen with ordinary unskilled laborers who worked one small task faster and more efficiently, cutting the time to make a Model T from twenty-one days to four days and cutting labor hours by 60 percent.[5] With lower costs, Ford was able to charge a price that was accessible to the mass market.

Sales of the Model T exploded. Ford's market share surged from 9 percent in 1908 to 61 percent in 1921, and by 1923, a majority of American households owned an automobile.[6] Ford's Model T exploded the size of the automobile industry, creating a huge blue ocean. So great was the blue ocean Ford created that the Model T replaced the horse-drawn carriage as the primary means of transport in the United States.

General Motors

By 1924, the car had become an essential household item, and the wealth of the average American household had grown. That year General Motors (GM) unveiled a line of automobiles that would create a new blue ocean in the auto industry. In contrast to Ford's functional, one-color, single-model strategy, GM introduced "a car for every purse and purpose"—a strategy devised by chairman Alfred Sloan to appeal to the emotional dimensions of the U.S. mass market, or what Sloan called the "mass-class" market.[7]

Whereas Ford stuck with the functional "horseless carriage" concept of the car, GM made the car fun, exciting, comfortable, and fashionable. GM factories pumped out a broad array of models, with new colors and styles updated every year. The "annual car model" created new demand as buyers began to trade up for fashion and comfort. Because cars were replaced more frequently, the used car market was also formed.

Demand for GM's fashionable and emotionally charged cars soared. From 1926 to 1950, the total number of cars sold in the United States increased from two million to seven million a year, and General Motors increased its overall market share from 20 percent to 50 percent, while Ford's fell from 50 percent to 20 percent.[8]

But the rapid growth in the U.S. auto industry unleashed by this new blue ocean could not last forever. Following GM's surging success, Ford and Chrysler jumped into the blue ocean GM had created, and the Big Three pursued the common strategy of launching new car models yearly and hitting an emotional chord with consumers by building a wide range of car styles to meet various lifestyles and needs. Slowly, bloody competition began as the Big Three imitated and matched one another's strategies. Collectively, they captured more than 90 percent of the U.S. auto market.[9] A period of complacency set in.

Small, Fuel-Efficient Japanese Cars

The auto industry, however, did not stand still. In the 1970s, the Japanese created a new blue ocean, challenging the U.S. automobile industry with small, efficient cars. Instead of following the implicit industry logic "the bigger, the better" and focusing on luxuries, the Japanese altered the conventional logic, pursuing ruthless quality, small size, and the new utility of highly gas-efficient cars.

When the oil crisis occurred in the 1970s, U.S. consumers flocked to fuel-efficient, robust Japanese cars made by Honda, Toyota, and Nissan (then called Datsun). Almost overnight the Japanese became heroes in consumers' minds. Their compact, fuel-efficient cars created a new blue ocean of opportunity, and again demand soared.

With the Big Three focused on benchmarking and matching one another, none had taken the initiative to produce functional, compact, fuel-efficient cars, even though they did see the market potential for such vehicles. Hence, instead of creating a new blue ocean, the Big Three were dragged into a new round of competitive benchmarking, only this time with the Japanese; they began to invest heavily in the production of smaller, fuel-efficient vehicles.

Nevertheless, the Big Three were still hit by a dive in car sales, with aggregate losses mounting to $4 billion in 1980.[10] Chrysler, the little brother among the Big Three, suffered the hardest hit and narrowly escaped bankruptcy by virtue of a government bailout. The Japanese car producers had been so effective at creating and capturing this blue ocean that the U.S. automakers found it hard to make a real comeback; their competitiveness and long-run viability were thrown into serious question by industry experts across the world.

Chrysler's Minivan

Fast-forward to 1984. A beleaguered Chrysler, on the edge of bankruptcy, unveiled the minivan, creating a new blue ocean in the auto industry. The minivan broke the boundary between car and van, creating an entirely new type of vehicle. Smaller than the traditional van and yet more spacious than the station wagon, the minivan was exactly what the nuclear family needed to hold the entire family plus its bikes, dogs, and other necessities. And the minivan was easier to drive than a truck or van.

Built on the Chrysler K car chassis, the minivan drove like a car but provided more interior room and could still fit in the family garage. Chrysler, however, was not the first to work on this concept. Ford and GM had had the minivan on their drawing boards for years, but they had worried that the design would cannibalize their own station wagons. Undoubtedly they passed a golden opportunity to Chrysler. Within its first year, the minivan became Chrysler's bestselling vehicle, helping the company regain its position as one of the Big Three auto manufacturers. Within three years, Chrysler gained $1.5 billion from the minivan's introduction alone.[11]

The success of the minivan ignited the sports utility vehicle (SUV) boom in the 1990s, which expanded the blue ocean Chrysler had unlocked. Built on a truck chassis, the SUV continued the progression from car to utility truck. First designed for off-road driving and towing boat trailers, the SUV became wildly popular with young families for its carlike handling, increased passenger and cargo space over the minivan, and comfortable interiors combined with the increased functionality of four-wheel drive, towing capabilities, and safety. By 1998, total sales of new light trucks (minivans, SUVs, and pickups) reached 7.5 million, nearly matching the 8.2 million new car sales.[12]

As history reveals, GM and Chrysler were established players when they created blue oceans. For the most part, however, these blue oceans were not triggered by technological innovations. The underlying technology had been around; even Ford's revolutionary assembly line can be traced to the U.S. meatpacking industry.[13] The attractiveness of the auto industry was continuously rising and falling and rising again, driven, to no small extent, by blue ocean strategic moves. The same is true for the profitable growth trends of companies in the industry. Companies' profit and growth were linked in no small way to the blue oceans they created or failed to create.

Almost all these companies are remembered for the blue oceans they have created across time. Ford, for example, has suffered significantly at times, but its brand still stands out largely for the Model T it created some one hundred years ago.

The Computer Industry

Let's now turn to the computer industry, which supplies a central component of work environments across the globe. The U.S. computer industry traces back to 1890, when Herman Hollerith invented the punch card tabulating machine to shorten the process of data recording and analysis for the U.S. census. Hollerith's tabulator completed the census tabulations five years sooner than the preceding census.

Soon after, Hollerith left the census office to form Tabulating Machine Company (TMC), which sold its tabulators to U.S. and foreign government agencies. At the time, there was no real market for Hollerith's tabulators in business settings, where data processing was accomplished with pencils and ledgers that were easy to use, inexpensive, and accurate. Although Hollerith's tabulator was very fast and accurate, it was expensive and difficult to use, and it required continuous upkeep. Facing new competition after the expiration of his patent and frustrated after the U.S. government dropped TMC due to its steep prices, Hollerith sold the company, which was then merged with two other companies to form CTR in 1911.

The Tabulating Machine

In 1914, CTR's tabulating business remained small and unprofitable. In an attempt to turn the company around, CTR turned to Thomas Watson, a former executive at National Cash Register Company, for help. Watson recognized that there was enormous untapped demand for tabulators to help businesses improve their inventory and accounting practices. Yet he also realized that the cumbersome new technology was too expensive and complicated for businesses when their pencils and ledgers worked just fine.

In a strategic move that would launch the computer industry, Watson combined the strengths of the tabulator with the ease and lower costs of pencils and ledgers. Under Watson, CTR's tabulators were simplified and modularized, and the company began to offer on-site maintenance and user education and oversight. Customers would get the speed and efficiency of the tabulator without the need to hire specialists to train employees or technicians to fix the machines when they broke down.

Next, Watson decreed that tabulators would be leased and not sold, an innovation that helped establish a new pricing model for the tabulating machine business. On the one hand, it allowed businesses to avoid large capital expenditures, while giving them the flexibility to upgrade as tabulators improved. On the other hand, it gave CTR a recurring revenue stream while precluding customers from buying used machines from one another.

Within six years, the firm's revenues more than tripled.[14] By the mid-1920s, CTR held 85 percent of the tabulating market in the United States. In 1924, to reflect the company's growing international presence, Watson changed CTR's name to International Business Machines Corp. (IBM). The blue ocean of tabulators was unlocked.

The Electronic Computer

Skip ahead thirty years to 1952. Remington Rand delivered the UNIVAC, the world's first commercial electronic computer, to the census bureau. Yet that year only three UNIVACs were sold. A blue ocean was not in sight until IBM's Watson—this time his son Thomas Watson Jr.—would see the untapped demand in what looked like a small, lackluster market. Watson Jr. realized the role electronic computers could play in business and pushed IBM to meet the challenge.

In 1953, IBM introduced the IBM 650, the first intermediate-sized computer for business use. Recognizing that if businesses were going to use the electronic computer, they wouldn't want a complicated machine and would pay only for the computing power they would use, IBM had made the IBM 650 much simpler to use and less powerful than the UNIVAC, and it priced the machine at only $200,000, compared with the UNIVAC's $1 million price tag. As a result, by the end of the 1950s IBM had captured 85 percent of the business electronic computer market. Revenues almost tripled between 1952 and 1959, from $412 million to $1.16 billion.[15]

IBM's expansion of the blue ocean was greatly accentuated in 1964, with the introduction of the System/360, the first large family of computers to use interchangeable software, peripheral equipment, and service packages. It was a bold departure from the monolithic, one-size-fits-all mainframe. Later, in 1969, IBM changed the way computers were sold. Rather than offer hardware, services, and software exclusively in packages, IBM unbundled the components and offered them for sale individually. Unbundling gave birth to the multibillion-dollar software and services industries. Today, IBM is the world's largest computer services company, and it remains the world's largest computer manufacturer.

The Personal Computer

The computer industry continued its evolution through the 1960s and 1970s. IBM, Digital Equipment Corporation (DEC), Sperry, and others that had jumped into the computer industry expanded operations globally and improved and extended product lines to add peripherals and service markets. Yet in 1978, when the major computer manufacturers were intent on building bigger, more powerful machines for the business market, Apple Computer, Inc., created an entirely new market space with its Apple II home computer.

However, contrary to conventional wisdom, the Apple was not the first personal computer on the market. Two years earlier, Micro Instrumentation and Telemetry Systems (MITS) had unveiled the Altair 8800. The Altair was released with high expectations in computer hobbyist circles. *BusinessWeek* quickly called MITS the "IBM of home computers."

Yet MITS did not create a blue ocean. Why? The machine had no monitor, no permanent memory, only 256 characters of temporary memory, no software, and no keyboard. To enter data, users manipulated switches on the front of the box, and program results were displayed in a pattern of flashing lights on the front panel. Unsurprisingly, no one saw much of a market for such difficult-to-use home computers. Expectations were so low that in that same year Ken Olsen, president of Digital Equipment, famously said, "There is no reason for any individual to have a computer in their home."

Two years later, the Apple II would make Olsen eat his words, creating a blue ocean of home computing. Based largely on existing technology, the Apple II offered a solution with an all-in-one design in a plastic casing, including the keyboard, power supply, and graphics, that was easy to use. The Apple II came with software ranging from games to businesses programs such as the Apple Writer word processor and the VisiCalc spreadsheet, making the computer accessible to the mass of buyers.

Apple changed the way people thought about computers. Computers were no longer products for technological "geeks"; they became, like the Model T before them, a staple of the American household. Only two years after the birth of the Apple II, Apple sales were more than 200,000 units a year, with Apple placed on the *Fortune* 500 list at three years of age, an unprecedented feat.[16] In 1980 some two dozen firms sold 724,000 personal computers, bringing in more than $1.8 billion.[17] By the next year, twenty other companies entered the market, and sales doubled to 1.4 million units, racking in almost $3 billion.[18]

Like a stalking horse, IBM waited out the first couple of years to study the market and the technology and to plan the launch of its home computer. In 1982, IBM dramatically expanded the blue ocean of home computing by offering a far more open architecture that allowed other parties to write software and develop peripherals. By creating a standardized operating system for which outsiders could create the software and peripheral components, IBM was able to keep its cost and price low while offering customers greater utility. The company's scale and scope advantages allowed it to price its PC at a level accessible to the mass of buyers.[19] During its first year, IBM sold 200,000 PCs, nearly matching its five-year projection; by 1983 consumers had bought 1.3 million IBM PCs.[20]

Compaq PC Servers

With corporations across the United States buying and installing PCs throughout their organizations, there was a growing need to connect PCs for simple but important tasks such as sharing files and printers. The business computer industry spawned by the IBM 650—and jumped into by HP, DEC, and Sequent, to name a few— offered high-end enterprise systems to run corporations' critical missions, as well as numerous operating systems and application software. But these machines were too expensive and complex to justify handling simple but important needs such as file and printer sharing. This was especially true in small to midsize companies that needed to share printers and files but did not yet require the huge investment of a complex minicomputer architecture.

In 1992, Compaq changed all that by effectively creating the blue ocean of the PC server industry with its launch of the ProSignia, a radically simplified server that was optimized for the most commonly used functions of file and printer sharing. It eliminated interoperability with a host of operating systems, ranging from SCO UNIX to OS/3 to DOS, that were extraneous to these basic functions. The new PC server gave buyers twice a minicomputer's file and print sharing capability and speed at one-third the price. As for Compaq, the dramatically simplified machines translated into much lower manufacturing costs. Compaq's creation of the ProSignia, and three subsequent offerings in the PC server industry, not only fueled PC sales but also grew the PC server industry into a $3.8 billion industry in less than four years.[21]

Dell Computer

In the mid-1990s, Dell Computer Corporation created another blue ocean in the computer industry. Traditionally, computer manufactures competed on offering faster computers having more features and software. Dell, however, challenged this industry logic by changing the purchasing and delivery experiences of buyers. With its direct sales to customers, Dell was able to sell its PCs for 40 percent less than IBM dealers while still making money.

Direct sales further appealed to customers because Dell offered unprecedented delivery time. For example, the time it took from order to customer delivery at Dell was four days, compared with its competitors' average of more than ten weeks. Moreover, through Dell's online and telephone ordering system, customers were given the option to customize their machines to their liking. In the meantime, the built-to-order model allowed Dell to significantly reduce inventory costs.

Today Dell is the undisputed market leader in PC sales, with revenues skyrocketing from $5.3 billion in 1995 to $35.5 billion in 2003. Its U.S. market share grew from 2 percent to more than 30 percent in the same period.[22]

As with the auto industry, the blue oceans in the computer industry were not unleashed by technology innovations per se but by linking technology to elements valued by buyers. As in the case of the IBM 650 and the Compaq PC server, the value innovation often rested on simplifying the technology. We also see industry incumbents—CTR, IBM, Compaq—launching blue oceans as much as we see new entrants, such as Apple and Dell. Each blue ocean has reinforced the originating company's standing brand name and has led to a surge not only in its profitable growth but in the profitable growth of the computer industry overall.

The Movie Theater Industry

Now let's turn to the movie theater industry, which offers a way for many of us to relax after work or on weekends. The U.S. movie theater industry can be traced back to 1893, when Thomas Edison unveiled the Kinetoscope, a wooden cabinet inside which light was projected through a reel of film. Viewers saw the action through a peephole one at a time, and the performance was called a "peep show."

Two years later, Edison's staff developed a projecting kinetoscope, which showed motion pictures on a screen. The projecting kinetoscope, however, did not take off in any meaningful way. The clips, each several minutes long, were introduced between vaudeville acts and at theaters. The aim was to lift the value of live entertainment performances, the focus of the theater industry, rather than to provide a discrete entertainment form. The technology was there for the movie theater industry to ignite, but the idea to create a blue ocean had not yet been planted.

Nickelodeons

Harry Davis changed all that by opening his first nickelodeon theater in Pittsburgh, Pennsylvania, in 1905. The nickelodeon is widely credited with launching the movie theater industry in the United States, creating a huge blue ocean. Consider the differences. Although most Americans belonged to the working class at the beginning of the twentieth century, the theater industry until then concentrated on offering live entertainment, such as theater, operas, and vaudeville, to the social elite.

With the average family earning only $12 a week, live entertainment simply wasn't an option. It was too expensive. Average ticket prices for an opera were $2, and vaudeville was 50 cents. For the majority, theater was too serious. With little education, the theater or opera just wasn't appealing to the working class. It was also inconvenient. Productions played only a few times a week, and with most theaters located in the well-heeled parts of the city, they were difficult to get to for the mass of working-class people. When it came to entertainment, most Americans were left in the dark.

In contrast, the price of admission to Davis's nickelodeon theater was 5 cents (thus explaining the name). Davis kept the price at a nickel by stripping the theater venue to its bare essentials—benches and the screen—and placing his theaters in lower-rent, working-class neighborhoods. Next he focused on volume and convenience, opening his theaters at eight in the morning and playing reels continuously until midnight. The nickelodeons were fun, playing slapstick comedies accessible to most people regardless of their education, language, or age.

Working-class people flocked to nickelodeons, which entertained some seven thousand customers per day. In 1907 the *Saturday Evening Post* reported that daily attendance at nickelodeons exceeded two million.[23] Soon nickelodeons set up shop across the country. By 1914 the United States had eighteen thousand nickelodeons, with seven million daily admissions.[24] The blue ocean had grown into a half-billion-dollar industry.

The Palace Theaters

As the nickelodeon's blue ocean reached its peak, in 1914 Samuel "Roxy" Rothapfel set out to bring the appeal of motion pictures to the emerging middle and upper classes by opening the country's first Palace Theater in New York City. Until that point, Rothapfel had owned a number of nickelodeons in the United States and was best known for turning around struggling theaters across the country. Unlike nickelodeons, which were considered lowbrow and simplistic, Rothapfel's Palace Theaters were elaborate affairs, with extravagant chandeliers, mirrored hallways, and grand entranceways. With valet parking, plush "love seats," and longer films with theatrical plots, these theaters made going to the movies an event worthy of theater- or operagoers, but at an affordable price.

The picture palaces were a commercial success. Between 1914 and 1922, four thousand new Palace Theaters opened in the United States. Movie-going became an increasingly important entertainment event for Americans of all economic levels. As Roxy pointed out, "Giving the people what they want is fundamentally and disastrously wrong. The people don't know what they want . . . [Give] them something better." Palace Theaters effectively combined the viewing environment of opera houses with the viewing contents of nickelodeons—films—to unlock a new blue ocean in the cinema industry and attract a whole new mass of moviegoers: the upper and middle classes.[25]

As the wealth of the nation increased and Americans headed for the suburbs to fulfill the dream of a house with a picket fence, a chicken in every pot, and a car in every garage, the limitations of further growth in the Palace Theater concept began to be felt in the late 1940s. Suburbs, unlike major cities or metropolitan areas, could not support the large size and opulent interiors of the Palace Theater concept. The result of competitive evolution was the emergence of small theaters in suburban locations running one movie per week. Although the small theaters were "cost leaders" compared with Palace Theaters, they failed to capture people's imaginations. They gave people no special feeling of a night out, and their success depended solely on the quality of the film being played. If a film was unsuccessful, customers saw no reason to come, and the theater owner lost money. With the industry increasingly taking on a has-been status, its profitable growth was flagging.

The Multiplex

Yet, once again, the industry was set on a new profitable growth trajectory through the creation of a new blue ocean. In 1963, Stan Durwood undertook a strategic move that turned the industry on its head. Durwood's father had opened his family's first movie theater in Kansas City in the 1920s, and Stan Durwood revitalized the movie theater industry with the creation of the first multiplex in a Kansas City shopping center.

The multiplex was an instant hit. On the one hand, the multiplex gave viewers a greater choice of films; on the other, with different-sized theaters in one place, theater owners could make adjustments to meet varying demands for movies, thereby spreading their risk and keeping costs down. As a result, Durwood's company, American Multi-Cinema, Inc. (AMC), grew from a small-town theater to become the second largest movie company in the nation, as the blue ocean of the multiplex spread across America.

The Megaplex

The launch of the multiplex created a blue ocean of new profitable growth in the industry, but by the 1980s the spread of videocassette recorders and satellite and cable television had reduced movie attendance. To make matters worse, in an attempt to capture a greater share of a shrinking market, theater owners split their theaters into smaller and smaller viewing rooms so that they could show more features. Unwittingly, they undermined one of the industry's distinctive strengths over home entertainment: large screens. With first-run movies available on cable and videocassette only weeks after release, the benefit of paying more money to see movies on a slightly larger screen was marginal. The movie theater industry fell into a steep decline.

In 1995, AMC again re-created the movie theater industry by introducing the first twenty-four-screen megaplex in the United States. Unlike the multiplexes, which were often cramped, dingy, and unspectacular, the megaplex had stadium seating (for unobstructed views) and comfortable easy chairs, and it offered more films and superior sight and sound. Despite these improved offerings, the megaplex's operating costs are still lower than the multiplex's. This is because the megaplex's location outside city centers—the key cost factor—is much cheaper; its size gives it economies in purchasing and operations and more leverage with film distributors. And with twenty-four screens playing every available movie on the market, the place, and not the movie, becomes the draw.

In the late 1990s, average per-customer revenues at AMC megaplexes were 8.8 percent above those of the average multiplex theater. The cinema clearance zones of movie theaters—the radius of the area from which people will come to the cinema—jumped from two miles in the mid-1990s to five miles for AMC's megaplex.[26] Between 1995 and 2001, overall motion picture attendance grew from 1.26 billion to 1.49 billion. Megaplexes constituted only 15 percent of U.S. movie screens, but they accounted for 38 percent of all box-office revenues.

The success of the blue ocean created by AMC caused other industry players to imitate it. Too many megaplexes were built in too short a time, however, and many of them had closed by 2000 because of a slowing economy. Again the industry is ripe for a new blue ocean to be created.

This is only a sketch of the American movie theater industry, but the same general patterns appear as in the other examples. This has not been a perpetually attractive industry. There has not been a perpetually excellent company. The creation of blue oceans has been a key driving factor in a company's and the industry's profitable growth trajectory, with blue oceans being created here mainly by incumbents such as AMC and Palace Theaters. As history reveals, AMC created a blue ocean in the U.S. movie theater industry first with the multiplex and then with megaplex, twice resetting the course of development for the entire industry and twice bringing its own profitability and growth to a new level. At the heart of these blue oceans was not technology innovation per se but value-driven innovation, what we call value innovation.

Looking across the sketches of these three industries we find that whether or not a company can attain sustained profitable growth depends largely on whether it can continuously stay in the forefront during consecutive rounds of blue ocean creation. Lasting excellence is scarcely achievable for any company; to date, no company has been able to lead journeys into blue oceans continuously over the long run. However, companies with powerful names are often those that have been capable of reinventing themselves by repeatedly creating new market space. In this sense, there have been no perpetually excellent companies up till now, but companies can hope to maintain excellence by adhering to excellent strategic practice. With marginal deviations, the pattern of blue ocean creation exemplified by these three representative industries is consistent with what we observed in the other industries in our study.

Value Innovation

A Reconstructionist View of Strategy

THERE ARE BASICALLY TWO DISTINCT VIEWS on how industry structure is related to strategic actions of industrial players.

The *structuralist* view of strategy has its roots in industrial organization (IO) economics.[1] The model of industrial organization analysis proposes a structure-conduct-performance paradigm, which suggests a causal flow from market structure to conduct and performance. *Market structure*, given by supply and demand conditions, shapes sellers' and buyers' *conduct,* which, in turn, determines *end performance.*[2] Systemwide changes are induced by factors that are external to the market structure, such as fundamental changes in basic economic conditions and technological breakthroughs.[3]

The *reconstructionist* view of strategy, on the other hand, is built on the theory of endogenous growth. The theory traces back to Joseph A. Schumpeter's initial observation that the forces that change economic structure and industry landscapes can come from *within* the system.[4] Schumpeter argues that innovation can happen endogenously and that its main source is the creative entrepreneur.[5] Schumpeterian innovation is still black-boxed, however, because it is the product of the ingenuity of entrepreneurs and cannot be reproduced systematically.

Recently, the *new growth theory* made advances on this front by showing that innovation can be replicable endogenously via an understanding of the patterns or recipes behind innovation.[6] In essence, this theoretical advancement separated the recipe for innovation—or the pattern of knowledge and ideas behind it—from Schumpeter's lone entrepreneur, opening the way for the systematic reproduction of innovation. However, despite this important advance, we still lack an understanding of what those recipes or patterns are. Absent this, knowledge and ideas cannot be deployed in action to produce innovation and growth at the firm level.

The reconstructionist view takes off where the new growth theory left off. Building on the new growth theory, the reconstructionist view suggests how knowledge and ideas are deployed in the process of creation to produce endogenous growth for the firm. In particular, it proposes that such a process of creation can occur in any organization at any time by the cognitive reconstruction of existing data and market elements in a fundamentally new way.

These two views—the structuralist and the reconstructionist—have important implications for how companies act on strategy. The structuralist view (or environmental determinism) often leads to competition-based strategic thinking. Taking market structure as given, it drives companies to try to carve out a defensible position against the competition in the existing market space. To sustain themselves in the marketplace, practitioners of strategy focus on building advantages over the competition, usually by assessing what competitors do and striving to do it better. Here, grabbing a bigger share of the market is seen as a zero-sum game in which one company's gain is achieved at another company's loss. Hence, competition, the supply side of the equation, becomes the defining variable of strategy.

Such strategic thinking leads firms to divide industries into attractive and unattractive ones and to decide accordingly whether or not to enter. After it is in an industry, a firm chooses a distinctive cost or differentiation position that best matches its internal systems and capabilities to counter the competition.[7] Here, cost and value are seen as trade-offs. Because the total profit level of the industry is also determined exogenously by structural factors, firms principally seek to capture and redistribute wealth instead of creating wealth. They focus on dividing up the red ocean, where growth is increasingly limited.

To reconstructionist eyes, however, the strategic challenge looks very different. Recognizing that structure and market boundaries exist only in managers' minds, practitioners who hold this view do not let existing market structures limit their thinking. To them, extra demand is out there, largely untapped. The crux of the problem is how to create it. This, in turn, requires a shift of attention from supply to demand, from a focus on competing to a focus on value innovation—that is, the creation of innovative value to unlock new demand. With this new focus in mind, firms can hope to accomplish the journey of discovery by looking systematically across established boundaries of competition and reordering existing elements in different markets to reconstruct them into a new market space where a new level of demand is generated.[8]

In the reconstructionist view, there is scarcely any attractive or unattractive industry per se because the level of industry attractiveness can be altered through companies' conscientious efforts of reconstruction. As market structure is changed in the reconstruction process, so are best-practice rules of the game. Competition in the old game is therefore rendered irrelevant. By stimulating the demand side of the economy, the strategy of value innovation expands existing markets and creates new ones. Value innovators achieve a leap in value by creating new wealth rather than at the expense of competitors in the traditional sense. Such a strategy therefore allows firms to largely play a non–zero-sum game, with high payoff possibilities.

How, then, does reconstruction, such as what we see in Cirque du Soleil, differ from the "combination" and "recombination" that have been discussed in the innovation literature?[9] Schumpeter, for example, sees innovation as a "new combination of productive means."

We have seen in the example of Cirque du Soleil a focus on the demand side, whereas recombination is about recombining existing technologies or productive means, often focusing on the supply side. The basic building blocks for reconstruction are *buyer value elements* that reside across existing industry boundaries. They are not *technologies* nor *methods of production*.

By focusing on the supply side, recombination tends to seek an innovative solution to the existing problem. Looking at the demand side, in contrast, reconstruction breaks away from the cognitive bounds set by existing rules of competition. It focuses on redefining the existing problem itself. Cirque du Soleil, for example, is not about offering a *better circus* by recombining existing knowledge or technologies about acts and performances. Rather, it is about reconstructing existing buyer value elements to create a new form of entertainment that offers the fun and thrill of the circus with the intellectual sophistication of the theater. Redefining the problem usually leads to changes in the entire system and hence a shift in strategy, whereas recombination may end up finding new solutions to subsystem activities that serve to reinforce an existing strategic position.

Reconstruction reshapes the boundary and the structure of an industry and creates a blue ocean of new market space. Recombination, on the other hand, tends to maximize technological possibilities to discover innovative solutions.

The Market Dynamics
of Value Innovation

THE MARKET DYNAMICS of value innovation stand in stark contrast with the conventional practice of technology innovation. The latter typically sets high prices, limits access, and initially engages in price skimming to earn a premium on the innovation, only later focusing on lowering prices and costs to retain market share and discourage imitators.

However, in a world of nonrival and nonexcludable goods, such as knowledge and ideas, that are imbued with the potential of economies of scale, learning, and increasing returns, the importance of volume, price, and cost grows in an unprecedented way.[1] Under these conditions, companies would do well to capture the mass of target buyers from the outset and expand the size of the market by offering radically superior value at price points accessible to them.

As shown in Figure C-1, value innovation radically increases the appeal of a good, shifting the demand curve from D1 to D2. The

FIGURE C-1

The Market Dynamics of Value Innovation

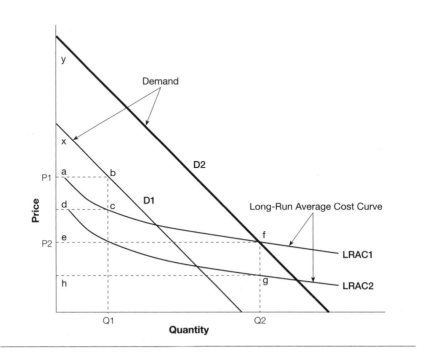

price is set strategically and, as with the Swatch example, is shifted from P1 to P2 to capture the mass of buyers in the expanded market. This increases the quantity sold from Q1 to Q2 and builds strong brand recognition, for unprecedented value.

The company, however, engages in target costing to simultaneously reduce the long-run average cost curve from LRAC1 to LRAC2 to expand its ability to profit and to discourage free riding and imitation. Hence, buyers receive a leap in value, shifting the consumer surplus from axb to eyf. And the company earns a leap in profit and growth, shifting the profit zone from abcd to efgh.

The rapid brand recognition built by the company as a result of the unprecedented value offered in the marketplace, combined with the simultaneous drive to lower costs, makes the competition nearly irrelevant and makes it hard to catch up, as economies of scale, learning, and increasing returns kick in. What follows is the emergence of win-win market dynamics, where companies earn dominant positions while buyers also come out big winners.

Traditionally, firms with monopolistic positions have been associated with two social welfare loss activities. First, to maximize their profits, companies set prices high. This prohibits those customers who, although desiring the product, cannot afford to buy it. Second, lacking viable competition, firms with monopolistic positions often do not focus on efficiency and cost reduction and hence consume more scarce resources. As Figure C-2 shows, under conventional monopolistic practice, the price level is raised from P1 under perfect competition to P2 under monopoly. Consequently, demand drops from Q1 to Q2. At this level of demand, the monopolist increases its profits by the area R, as opposed to the situation of perfect competition. Because of the artificially high price imposed on consumers, the consumer surplus decreases from area C+R+D to area C. Meanwhile, the monopolistic practice, by consuming more of the society's resources, also incurs a deadweight loss of

FIGURE C-2

From Perfect Competition to Monopolist Practice

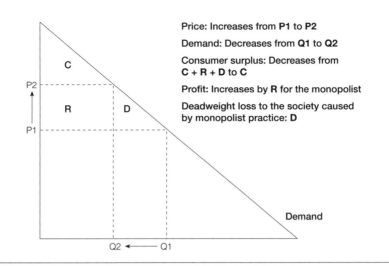

Price: Increases from **P1** to **P2**

Demand: Decreases from **Q1** to **Q2**

Consumer surplus: Decreases from **C + R + D** to **C**

Profit: Increases by **R** for the monopolist

Deadweight loss to the society caused by monopolist practice: **D** area D for the society at large. Monopolistic profits, therefore, are achieved at the expense of consumers and society at large.

Blue ocean strategy, on the other hand, works against this sort of price skimming, which is common to traditional monopolists. The focus of blue ocean strategy is not on restricting output at a high price but rather on creating new aggregate demand through a leap in buyer value at an accessible price. This creates a strong incentive not only to reduce costs to the lowest possible level at the start but also to keep it that way over time to discourage potential free-riding imitators. In this way, buyers win and the society benefits from improved efficiency. This creates a win-win scenario. A breakthrough in value is achieved for buyers, for the company, and for society at large.

Notes

Chapter 1

1. For discussions on how market boundaries are defined and how competitive rules of the game are set, see Harrison C. White (1981) and Joseph Porac and José Antonio Rosa (1996).

2. Gary Hamel and C. K. Prahalad (1994) and James Moore (1996) observed that competition is intensifying and commoditization of business is accelerating, two trends that make market creation essential if firms are to grow.

3. Ever since the groundbreaking work of Michael Porter (1980, 1985), competition has occupied the center of strategic thinking. See also Paul Auerbach (1988) and George S. Day et al. (1997).

4. See, for example, Hamel and Prahalad (1994).

5. See *Standard Industrial Classification Manual* (1987) and *North American Industry Classification System* (1998).

6. Ibid.

7. For a classic on military strategy and its fundamental focus on competition over a limited territory, see Carl von Clausewitz (1993).

8. For discussions on this, see Richard A. D'Aveni and Robert Gunther (1995).

9. For more on globalization and its economic implications, see Kenichi Ohmae (1990, 1995a, 1995b).

10. United Nations Statistics Division (2002).

11. See, for example, Copernicus and Market Facts (2001).

12. Ibid.

13. Thomas J. Peters and Robert H. Waterman Jr. (1982) and Jim Collins and Jerry Porras (1994), respectively.

14. Richard T. Pascale (1990).

15. Richard Foster and Sarah Kaplan (2001).

16. Peter Drucker (1985) observes that companies tend to race against each other by looking at what competitors do.

17. Kim and Mauborgne (1997a, 1997b, 1997c) argue that a focus on benchmarking and beating the competition leads to imitative, not innovative, approaches to the market, often resulting in price pressure and further commodization. Instead, they argue, companies should strive to make the competition irrelevant by offering buyers a leap in value. Gary Hamel (1998) argues that success for both newcomers and industry incumbents hinges upon the capacity to avoid the competition and to reconceive the existing industry model. He further argues (2000) that the formula for success is not to position against the competition but rather to go around it.

18. Value creation as a concept of strategy is too broad, because no boundary condition specifies how value should be created. A company could create value, for example, simply by lowering costs by 2 percent. Although this is indeed value creation, it is hardly the value innovation that is needed to open new market space. Although you can create value by simply doing similar things in an improved way, you cannot create value innovation without stopping old things, doing new things, or doing similar things in a fundamentally new way. Our research shows that given the strategic objective of value creation, companies tend to focus on making incremental improvements at the margin. Although value creation on an incremental scale does create some value, it is not sufficient to make a company stand out in the crowd and achieve high performance.

19. For examples of market pioneering that shoots beyond what buyers are ready to accept and pay for, see Gerard J. Tellis and Peter N. Golder (2002). In their decade-long study they observe that fewer than 10 percent of market pioneers became business winners, with more than 90 percent turning out to be business losers.

20. For previous studies that challenged this dogma, see, for example, Charles W. L. Hill (1988) as well as R. E. White (1986).

21. For discussions on the necessity to choose between differentiation and low cost, see Porter (1980, 1985). Porter (1996) uses a productivity frontier curve to illustrate the value-cost trade-off.

22. Our studies revealed that value innovation is about redefining the problem an industry focuses on rather than finding solutions to existing problems.

23. For discussions on what strategy is and is not, see Porter (1996). He argues that although strategy should embrace the entire system of activities a firm performs, operational improvements can occur at the subsystem level.

24. Ibid. Hence, innovations that happen at the subsystem level are not strategy.

25. Joe S. Bain is a forerunner of the structuralist view. See Bain (1956, 1959).

26. Although in different contexts, venturing into the new has been observed to be a risky enterprise. Steven P. Schnaars (1994), for example, observes that market pioneers occupy a disadvantaged position vis-à-vis their imitators. Chris Zook (2004) argues that diversification away from a company's core business is risky and has low odds of success.

27. Inga S. Baird and Howard Thomas (1990) argue, for example, that any strategic decisions involve risk taking.

Chapter 2

1. Alternatives go beyond substitutes. A restaurant, for example, is an alternative to the cinema. It competes for potential buyers who want to enjoy a night out, even though it is neither a direct competitor nor a substitute for the cinema in its functional offering. There are three tiers of noncustomers a company can look to. For more detailed discussions on alternatives and noncustomers, see chapter 3 and chapter 5 of this book, respectively.

Chapter 3

1. NetJets (2004).
2. J. Balmer (2001).
3. Available online at http://www.marquisjet.com/vs/vscomm.html.
4. Kris Herbst (2002).
5. Ibid.

Chapter 4

1. For an overview of strategic planning, see Henry Mintzberg (1994).

2. Consider the difference in our perceptual bandwidth (bits/second) of the various senses: taste (1,000 bits/second); smell (100,000); hearing (100,000); touch (1,000,000); seeing (10,000,000). Source: T. Norretranders (1998). For further reading on the power of visual communication, see A. D. Baddely (1990), J. Larkin and H. Simon (1987), P. Lester (2000), and E. R.Tufte (1982).

3. For more on the power of experiential learning, see L. Borzak (1981) and D. A. Kolb (1983).

4. See chapter 3 for further discussion on how Bloomberg applied one of the six paths to blue ocean creation to break from the competition.

5. See chapter 5 for a discussion on noncustomers.

6. See chapter 3 for a thorough discussion of the six path framework applied here.

7. See *Korea Economic Daily* (2004).

Chapter 5

1. See Committee on Defense Manufacturing (1996), James Fallows (2002), and John Birkler et al. (2001).

2. Department of Defense (1993).

3. For more on the specifics of the JSF, see Bill Breen (2002), Fallows (2002), Federation of Atomic Scientists (2001), David H. Freedman (2002), *Nova* (2003), and United States Air Force (2002).

4. Given the almost ten-year time lag from the conception of the JSF F-35 strategy to its realization in 2010, we would argue that its success is in no way secured. As heads of the military and Pentagon change during this time, the challenge will be to hold tight to the JSF's value curve. It is essential not to slip into the "defense deal spiral" of behind-the-scenes bargaining for "just a little more" customization and, with it, ballooning costs and a resultant blurred value curve. To avoid this, the Pentagon, in conjunction with Lockheed Martin, will have to ensure that each branch of the military adheres to the strategic profile agreed to in the strategy canvas of JSF F-35. So far, it looks good, but the military cannot afford to relax. This is an ongoing mission.

Chapter 6

1. Rohlfs (1974) was the first to define and discuss network externalities. For a survey of recent work on this, see Katz and Shapiro (1994).

2. See Kenneth J. Arrow (1962) and Paul Romer (1990). It is worth noting that both Arrow and Romer limited their discussion of nonrival and nonexcludable goods to technological innovations, as is the tradition in economics. When the concept of innovation is redefined as value innovation, which is more relevant at the microeconomic firm level, the importance of the nonrival and nonexcludable notion is even more striking. This is because technological innovation often has a greater excludable component due to the possibility and relative ease of obtaining patent protection.

3. See Ford Motor Company (1924) and William J. Abernathy and Kenneth Wayne (1974).

Chapter 7

1. *New York Post* (1990).

2. The first application of the term *tipping points* to social behavior was in a 1957 study of racial segregation by Morton Grodzins (1957) and was more fully developed by University of Maryland economist Thomas

Schelling (1978). Most recently, Malcom Gladwell's book *The Tipping Point* (2000) popularized the notion and brought the term further into the common vernacular.

3. See Joseph Ledoux (1998) and J. S. Morris et al. (1998).

4. See Baddely (1990) and Kolb (1983).

5. See James Q. Wilson and George L. Kelling (1982) for a discussion on the theory of broken windows.

Chapter 8

1. Thibault and L. Walker (1975).

2. Subsequent researchers, such as Tom R. Tyler and E. Allan Lind, demonstrated the power of fair process across diverse cultures and social settings. See E. A. Lind and T. R. Tyler (1988) for their research and an overview of related work.

3. For a discussion on voluntary cooperation, see C. O'Reilly and J. Chatman (1986), D. Katz (1964), and P. M. Blau (1964).

4. See discussions in F. Herzberg (1966).

Appendix A

1. For a discussion of "creative destruction," see Joseph A. Schumpeter (1934; 1975).

2. *New York Times* (1906).

3. *Literary Digest* (1899).

4. Bruce McCalley (2002).

5. William J. Abernathy and Kenneth Wayne (1974).

6. Antique Automobile Club of America (2002).

7. Alfred P. Sloan (1965): 150.

8. Mariana Mazzucato and Willi Semmler (1998).

9. Lawrence J. White (1971).

10. *Economist* (1981).

11. Sanghoon Ahn (2002).

12. Walter Adams and James W. Brock (2001), Table 5.1, Figure 5-1: 116–117.

13. Andrew Hargadon (2003): 43.

14. International Business Machines (2002).

15. Regis McKenna (1989): 24.

16. *A+ Magazine* (1987): 48–49; *Fortune* (1982).

17. Otto Friedrich (1983).

18. Ibid.

19. The IBM was priced a little more than the Apple ($1,565 versus $1,200), but it included a monitor, and the Apple did not.

20. History of Computing Project (accessed 28 June 2002).

21. *Financial Times* (1999).

22. Hoovers Online (accessed 14 March 2003).

23. Digital History (2004).

24. Screen Source (2002).

25. Interestingly, a 1924 poll asked moviegoers what aspects of a cinema appealed to them most; 28 percent cited the music, 19 percent the courtesy of the staff, 19 percent the comfort of the interior, and 15 percent the attractiveness of the theater. Only 10 percent mentioned the films (R. Koszarski, 1990). And 24 percent of exhibitors surveyed in 1922 said that the quality of the feature film "made absolutely no difference" to success at the box office; what mattered, they said, was the surrounding program (ibid.). In fact, cinema advertisements at the time tended to give as much print to the music as they did to the films. With the introduction of sound technology in films in 1926, the importance of live music at the cinema (a band or orchestra and the associated costs) was dramatically reduced. Palace Theaters, with their elaborate décor, luxurious environment, and services such as valet parking, were well placed to take advantage of this shift for more than ten years, until Americans began heading to small-town suburbs in droves following World War II.

26. Screen Source (2002).

Appendix B

1. The structuralist school of IO economics finds its origin in Joe S. Bain's structure-conduct-performance paradigm. Using a cross-industry empirical framework, Bain focuses mainly on the impact of structure on performance. For more discussions on this, see Bain (1956, 1959).

2. F. M. Scherer builds on Bain's work and seeks to spell out the causal path between "structure" and "performance" by using "conduct" as an intervening variable. For more discussions, see Scherer (1970).

3. Ibid.

4. See Joseph A. Schumpeter (1975).

5. Ibid.

6. For more discussions on the new growth theory and endogenous growth, see Paul Romer (1990, 1994) and G. M. Grossman and E. Helpman (1995).

7. For detailed discussions on competitive strategy, see Porter (1980, 1985, 1996).

8. See Kim and Mauborgne (1997a, 1999a, 1999b).

9. See Joseph Schumpeter (1934) and Andrew Hargadon (2003).

Appendix C

1. For discussion on the potential of increasing returns, see Paul Romer (1986) and W. B. Arthur (1996).

Bibliography

A+ Magazine. 1987. "Back In Time." February, 48–49.

Abernathy, William J., and Kenneth Wayne. 1974. "Limits to the Learning Curve." *Harvard Business Review* 52, 109–120.

Adams, Walter, and James W. Brock. 2001. *The Structure of American Industry*. 10th edition. Princeton, NJ: Prentice Hall.

Ahn, Sanghoon. 2002. "Competition, Innovation, and Productivity Growth: A Review of Theory and Evidence." OECD Working Paper 20.

Andrews, Kenneth R. 1971. *The Concept of Corporate Strategy*. Homewood, IL: Irwin.

Ansoff, H. Igor. 1965. *Corporate Strategy: An Analytic Approach to Business Policy for Growth and Expansion*. New York: McGraw Hill.

Antique Automobile Club of America. 2002. *Automotive History—A Chronological History*. <http://www.aaca.org/history>. Accessed 18 June 2002.

Arrow, Kenneth J. 1962. "Economic Welfare and the Allocation of Resources for Inventions," in *The Rate and Direction of Inventive Activity*, edited by R. R. Nelson. Princeton, NJ: Princeton University Press, 609–626.

Arthur, W. B. 1996. "Increasing Returns and the New World of Business." *Harvard Business Review* 74, July–August, 100–109.

Auerbach, Paul. 1988. *Competition: The Economics of Industrial Change*. Cambridge: Basil Blackwell.

Baddely, A. D. 1990. *Human Memory: Theory and Practice*. Needham Heights, MA: Allyn & Bacon.

Bain, Joe S. 1956. *Barriers to New Competition: Their Character and Consequences in Manufacturing Industries*. Cambridge, MA: Harvard University Press.

Bain, Joe S., ed. 1959. *Industrial Organization.* New York: Wiley.

Baird, Inga S., and Howard Thomas. 1990. "What Is Risk Anyway? Using and Measuring Risk in Strategic Management," in *Risk, Strategy, and Management,* edited by Richard A. Bettis and Howard Thomas. Greenwich, CT: JAI Press Inc.

Balmer, J. 2001. "The New Jet Set." *Barron's* 19, November.

Bettis, Richard A., and Howard Thomas, eds. 1990. *Risk, Strategy, and Management.* Greenwich, CT: JAI Press Inc.

Birkler, J., et al. 2001. "Assessing Competitive Strategies for the Joint Strike Fighter: Opportunities and Options." Santa Monica, CA: Rand Corporation.

Blau, P. M. 1964. *Exchange and Power in Social Life.* New York: Wiley.

Borzak, L., ed. 1981. *Field Study: A Source Book for Experiential Learning.* Beverly Hills, CA: Sage Publications.

Breen, Bill. 2002. "High Stakes, Big Bets." *Fast Company,* April.

Chandler, Alfred. 1962. *Strategy and Structure: Chapters in the History of the Industrial Enterprise.* Cambridge, MA: The MIT Press.

Christensen, Clayton M. 1997. *The Innovator's Dilemma: When New Technologies Caused Great Firms to Fail.* Boston: Harvard Business School Press.

Collins, Jim, and Jerry Porras. 1994. *Built to Last.* New York: Harper Business.

Committee on Defense Manufacturing in 2010 and Beyond. 1996. *Defense Manufacturing in 2010 and Beyond.* Washington, DC: National Academy Press.

Copernicus and Market Facts. 2001. *The Commoditization of Brands and Its Implications for Marketers.* Auburndale, MA: Copernicus Marketing Consulting.

D'Aveni, Richard A., and Robert Gunther. 1995. *Hypercompetitive Rivalries: Competing in Highly Dynamic Environments.* New York: Free Press.

Day, George S., and David J. Reibstein, with Robert Gunther, eds. 1997. *Wharton on Dynamic Competitive Strategy.* New York: John Wiley.

Department of Defense Press Conference. 1993. "DOD Bottom Up Review." *Reuter's Transcript Report,* 1 September.

Digital History. 2004. *Chronology of Film History.* <http://www.digitalhistory. uh.edu/historyonline/film_chron.cfm>. Accessed 4 February 2004.

Drucker, Peter F. 1985. *Innovation and Entrepreneurship: Practice and Principles.* London: William Heinemann.

———. 1992. *Managing for the Future: The 1990s and Beyond.* New York: Dutton.

Economist. 2000. "Apocalypse Now." 13 January.

———. 1981. "Detroit Moves the Metal." 15 August.

———. 2001. "A New Orbit." 12 July.

Fallows, James. 2002. "Uncle Sam Buys an Airplane." *Atlantic Monthly,* June.

Federation of Atomic Scientists. 2001. "F-35 Joint Strike Fighter." <http://www.fas.org/man/dod-101/sys/ac/f-35.htm>. Accessed 21 October 2002.

Financial Times. 1999. "Compaq Stays Top of Server Table." 3 February.

Ford Motor Company. 1924. *Factory Facts from Ford.* Detroit.

Fortune. 1982. "Fortune Double 500." June.

Foster, Richard, and Sarah Kaplan. 2001. *Creative Destruction.* New York: Doubleday.

Freedman, David H. 2002. "Inside the Joint Strike Fighter." *Business 2.0,* February.

Friedrich, Otto. 1983. "1982 Person of the Year: The Personal Computer." *Time.* <http://www.time.com/time/poy2000/archive/1982.html>. Accessed 30 June 2002.

Gladwell, Malcom. 2000. *The Tipping Point: How Little Things Can Make a Big Difference.* New York: Little Brown & Company.

Grodzins, Morton. 1957. "Metropolitan Segregation." *Scientific American* 197, October.

Grossman, G. M., and E. Helpman. 1995. *Innovation and Growth.* Cambridge, MA: The MIT Press.

Hamel, Gary, and C. K. Prahalad. 1994. *Competing for the Future.* Boston: Harvard Business School Press.

Hamel, Gary. 1998. "Opinion: Strategy Innovation and the Quest for Value." *MIT Sloan Management Review* 39, no. 2, 8.

————. 2000. *Leading the Revolution.* Boston: Harvard Business School Press.

Hargadon, Andrew. 2003. *How Breakthroughs Happen.* Boston: Harvard Business School Press.

Herbst, Kris. 2002. "Enabling the Poor to Build Housing: Cemex Combines Profit and Social Development." *Changemakers Journal,* September/October.

Herzberg, F. 1966. *Work and the Nature of Man.* Cleveland, OH: World Publishing.

Hill, Charles W. L. 1988. "Differentiation versus Low Cost or Differentiation and Low Cost." *Academy of Management Review* 13, July, 401–412.

Hindle, T. 1994. *Field Guide to Strategy.* Boston: The Economist Books.

History of Computing Project. "Univac." <http://www.thocp.net/hardware/univac.htm >. Accessed 28 June 2002.

Hofer, Charles W., and Dan Schendel. 1978. *Strategy Formulation: Analytical Concepts.* St. Paul, MN: West Publishing.

Hoovers Online. <http://www.hoovers.com/>. Accessed 14 March 2003.

International Business Machines. 2002. *IBM Highlights: 1885–1969.* <http://www-1.ibm.com/ibm/history/documents/pdf/1885-1969.pdf>. Accessed 23 May 2002.

Kanter, Rosabeth Moss. 1983. *The Change Masters: Innovation for Productivity in the American Corporation.* New York: Simon & Schuster.

Katz, D. 1964. "The Motivational Basis of Organizational Behavior." *Behavioral Science* 9, 131–146.

Katz, Michael, and Carl Shapiro. 1994. "Systems Competition and Network Effects." *Journal of Economic Perspectives* 8, no. 2, 93–115.

Kim, W. Chan, and Renée Mauborgne. 1993. "Procedural Justice, Attitudes and Subsidiary Top Management Compliance with Multinational's Corporate Strategic Decisions." *The Academy of Management Journal* 36, no. 3, 502–526.

———. 1996. "Procedural Justice and Manager's In-role and Extra-role Behavior." *Management Science* 42, April, 499–515.

———. 1997a. "Value Innovation: The Strategic Logic of High Growth." *Harvard Business Review* 75, January–February, 102–112.

———. 1997b. "On the Inside Track." *Financial Times,* 7 April.

———. 1997c. "When 'Competitive Advantage' Is Neither." *Wall Street Journal,* 21 April.

———. 1997d. "Fair Process: Managing in the Knowledge Economy." *Harvard Business Review* 75, July–August.

———. 1998. "Procedural Justice, Strategic Decision Making and the Knowledge Economy." *Strategic Management Journal,* April.

———. 1999a. "Creating New Market Space." *Harvard Business Review* 77, January–February, 83–93.

———. 1999b. "Strategy, Value Innovation, and the Knowledge Economy." *Sloan Management Review* 40, no. 3, Spring.

———. 2000. "Knowing a Winning Business Idea When You See One." *Harvard Business Review* 78, September–October, 129–141.

———. 2002. "Charting Your Company's Future." *Harvard Business Review* 80, June, 76–85.

———. 2003. "Tipping Point Leadership." *Harvard Business Review* 81, April, 60–69.

Kolb, D. A. 1983. *Experiential Learning: Experience as the Source of Learning and Development.* New York: Prentice Hall Press.

Korea Economic Daily. 2004. 20, 22, 27 April; 4, 6 May.

Koszarski, R. 1990. *An Evening's Entertainment: The Age of the Silent Feature Picture, 1915–1928.* New York: Scribner and Sons.

Kuhn, Thomas S. 1996. *The Structure of Scientific Revolutions.* Chicago: University of Chicago Press.

Larkin, J., and H. Simon. 1987. "Why a Diagram Is (Sometimes) Worth 10,000 Words." *Cognitive Science* 4, 317–345.

Ledoux, Joseph. 1998. *The Emotional Brain: The Mysterious Underpinnings of Emotional Life.* New York: Simon & Schuster.

Lester, P. 2000. *Visual Communication Images with Messages.* Second edition. Belmont, CA: Wadsworth Publishing Company.

Lind, E. A., and T. R. Tyler. 1988. *The Social Psychology of Procedural Justice.* New York: Plenum Press.

Literary Digest. 1899. 14 October.

Markides, Constantinos C. 1997. "Strategic Innovation." *Sloan Management Review*, Spring.

Mazzucato, Mariana, and Willi Semmler. 1998. "Market Share Instability and Stock Price Volatility during the Industry Life-cycle: US Automobile Industry." *Journal of Evolutionary Economics* 8, no. 4, 10.

McCalley, Bruce. 2002. *Model T Ford Encyclopedia, Model T Ford Club of America,* May. <http://www.mtfca.com/encyclo/index.htm>. Accessed 18 May 2002.

McKenna, Regis.1989. *Who's Afraid of Big Blue?* New York: Addison-Wesley.

Mintzberg, H. 1994. *The Rise and Fall of Strategic Planning: Reconceiving Roles for Planning, Plans, and Planners.* New York: Free Press.

Mintzberg, H., B. Ahlstrand, and J. Lampel. 1998. *Strategy Safari: A Guided Tour through the Wilds of Strategic Management.* New York: Prentice Hall.

Moore, James F. 1996. *The Death of Competition: Leadership and Strategy in the Age of Business Ecosystems.* New York: HarperBusiness.

Morris, J. S., et al. 1998. "Conscious and Unconscious Emotional Learning in the Human Amygdala." *Nature* 393, 467–470.

NetJets. 2004. "The Buyers Guide to Fractional Aircraft Ownership." <http://www.netjets.com>. Accessed 8 May 2004.

New York Post. 1990. "Dave Do Something." 7 September.

New York Times. 1906. "'Motorists Don't Make Socialists,' They Say." 4 March, 12.

Norretranders, T. 1998. *The User Illusion: Cutting Consciousness Down to Size.* New York: Penguin Press Science.

North American Industry Classification System: United States 1997. 1998. Lanham, VA: Bernan Press.

Nova. 2003. "Battle of the X-Planes." PBS. 4 February.

Ohmae, Kenichi. 1982. *The Mind of the Strategist: The Art of Japanese Business.* New York: McGraw-Hill.

———. 1990. *The Borderless World: Power and Strategy in the Interlinked Economy.* New York: HarperBusiness.

———. 1995a. *End of the Nation State: The Rise of Regional Economies.* New York: HarperCollins.

Ohmae, Kenichi, ed. 1995b. *The Evolving Global Economy: Making Sense of the New World Order.* Boston: Harvard Business School Press.

O'Reilly, C., and J. Chatman. 1986. "Organization Commitment and Psychological Attachment: The Effects of Compliance Identification, and Internationalization on Prosocial Behavior." *Journal of Applied Psychology* 71, 492–499.

Pascale, Richard T. 1990. *Managing on the Edge.* New York: Simon & Schuster.

Peters, Thomas J., and Robert H. Waterman Jr. 1982. *In Search of Excellence: Lessons from America's Best-Run Companies.* New York: Warner Books.

Phelps, Elizabeth A., et al. 2001. "Activation of the Left Amygdala to a Cognitive Representation of Fear." *Nature Neuroscience* 4, April, 437–441.

Porac, Joseph, and Jose Antonio Rosa. 1996. "Rivalry, Industry Models, and the Cognitive Embeddedness of the Comparable Firm." *Advances in Strategic Management* 13, 363–388.

Porter, Michael. E. 1980. *Competitive Strategy.* New York: Free Press.

———. 1985. *Competitive Advantage.* New York: Free Press.

———. 1996. "What Is Strategy?" *Harvard Business Review* 74, November–December.

Prahalad, C. K., and Gary Hamel. 1990. "The Core Competence of the Corporation." *Harvard Business Review* 68, no. 3, 79–91.

Rohlfs, Jeffrey. 1974. "A Theory of Interdependent Demand for a Communications Service." *Bell Journal of Economics* 5, no. 1, 16–37.

Romer, Paul M. 1986. "Increasing Returns and Long-Run Growth." *Journal of Political Economy* 94, October, 1002–1037.

———. 1990. "Endogenous Technological Change." *Journal of Political Economy* 98, October, S71–S102.

———. 1994. "The Origins of Endogenous Growth." *Journal of Economic Perspectives* 8, Winter, 3–22.

Schelling, Thomas C. 1978. *Micromotives and Macrobehavior.* New York: W. W. Norton and Co.

Scherer, F. M. 1970. *Industrial Market Structure and Economic Performance.* Chicago: Rand McNally.

———. 1984. *Innovation and Growth: Schumpeterian Perspectives.* Cambridge, MA: The MIT Press.

Schnaars, Steven P. 1994. *Managing Imitation Strategies: How Later Entrants Seize Markets from Pioneers.* New York: Free Press.

Schumpeter, Joseph A. 1934. *The Theory of Economic Development.* Cambridge, MA: Harvard University Press.

———. 1975 (originally published 1942). *Capitalism, Socialism and Democracy.* New York: Harper.

Screen Source. 2002. "US Movie Theater Facts." <http://www.amug.org/~scrnsrc/theater_facts.html>. Accessed 20 August 2002.

Sloan, Alfred. 1965. *My Years with General Motors.* London: Sidgwick & Jackson.

Standard Industrial Classification Manual. 1987. Paramus, NJ: Prentice Hall Information Services.

Tellis, G., and P. Golder. 2002. *Will and Vision.* New York: McGraw Hill.

Thibault, J., and L. Walker. 1975. *Procedural Justice: A Psychological Analysis.* Hillsdale, NJ: Erlbaum.

Tufte, E. R. 1982. *The Visual Display of Quantitative Information.* Cheshire, CT: Graphics Press.

United Nations Statistics Division. 2002. *The Population and Vital Statistics Report.*

United States Air Force. 2002. "JSF Program Whitepaper." <http://www.jast.mil.> Accessed 21 November 2003.

von Clausewitz, Carl. 1993. *On War.* Edited and translated by Michael Howard and Peter Paret. New York: Knopf.

von Hippel, Eric. 1988. *The Sources of Innovation.* New York: Oxford University Press.

White, Harrison C. 1981. "Where Do Markets Come From?" *American Journal of Sociology* 87, 517–547.

White, Lawrence J. 1971. *The Automotive Industry after 1945.* Cambridge, MA: Harvard University Press.

White, R. E. 1986. "Generic Business Strategies, Organizational Context and Performance: An Empirical Investigation." *Strategic Management Journal* 7, 217–231.

Wilson, James Q., and George L. Kelling. 1982. "Broken Windows." *Atlantic Monthly*, March, vol. 249, no. 3, 29.

Zook, Chris. 2004. *Beyond the Core: Expand Your Market Without Abandoning Your Roots.* Boston: Harvard Business School Press.

Index

About the Authors

W. Chan Kim is Cofounder and Codirector of the INSEAD Blue Ocean Strategy Institute and The Boston Consulting Group Bruce D. Henderson Chair Professor of Strategy and International Management at INSEAD, France (the world's second-largest business school). Prior to joining INSEAD, he was a professor at the University of Michigan Business School. He has served as a board member as well as an adviser for a number of multinational corporations in Europe, the United States and Asia Pacific. He is an advisory member for the European Union and is the Country Advisor to Malaysia. He was born in Korea.

Kim is a Fellow of the World Economic Forum. His *Harvard Business Review* articles, coauthored with Renée Mauborgne, are worldwide bestsellers and have sold over half a million reprints. Their Value Innovation and Fair Process articles were selected as among the best classic articles ever published in *Harvard Business Review*. They have coauthored articles in the *Wall Street Journal*, the *Wall Street Journal Europe*, the *New York Times*, the *Financial Times*, and the *Asian Wall Street Journal*, among others. Kim has published numerous articles on strategy and managing the multinational, which can be found in: *Academy of Management Journal, Management Science, Organization Science, Strategic Management Journal, Administrative Science Quarterly, Journal of International Business Studies, Harvard Business Review, Sloan Management Review*, and others. The *Journal of International Management* recognizes Kim as one of the world's most influential academic journal authors in global strategy.

Kim is a winner of the Eldridge Haynes Prize, awarded by the Academy of International Business and the Eldridge Haynes Memorial Trust of Business International, for the best original paper in the field of international business. Thinkers 50, the global ranking of management gurus, places Kim among the top ten most influential thinkers in 2007. Kim cofounded the Blue Ocean Strategy Network (BOSN), a global community of practice on the Blue Ocean Strategy family of concepts that he and Mauborgne created. BOSN embraces academics, consultants, executives, and government officers. Visit BOSN at: www.blueoceanstrategy.com.

Renée Mauborgne is Cofounder and Codirector of the INSEAD Blue Ocean Strategy Institute, INSEAD Distinguished Fellow, and a professor of strategy at INSEAD, France (the world's second-largest business school). She was born in the United States. Mauborgne is a Fellow of the World Economic Forum. Her *Harvard Business Review* articles, coauthored with W. Chan Kim, are worldwide bestsellers and have sold over half a million reprints. Their "Value Innovation" and "Fair Process" articles were selected as among the best classic articles ever published in *Harvard Business Review*. They have coauthored articles in the *Wall Street Journal*, the *Wall Street Journal Europe*, the *New York Times*, and the *Financial Times*, among others.

Mauborgne has published numerous articles on strategy and managing the multinational, which can be found in: *Academy of Management Journal, Management Science, Organization Science, Strategic Management Journal, Administrative Science Quarterly, Journal of International Business Studies, Harvard Business Review, Sloan Management Review*, and others. Mauborgne is a winner of the Eldridge Haynes Prize, awarded by the Academy of International Business and the Eldridge Haynes Memorial Trust of Business International, for the best original paper in the field of international business. Thinkers 50, the global ranking of management gurus, places Mauborgne among the top ten most influential thinkers in 2007. She was also selected as the highest-placed woman in 2007 on Thinkers 50. Mauborgne won the 2007 Asia Brand Leadership Award.

Mauborgne cofounded the Blue Ocean Strategy Network (BOSN), a global community of practice on the Blue Ocean Strategy family of concepts that she and Kim created. BOSN embraces academics, consultants, executives, and government officers. Visit BOSN at: www.blueoceanstrategy.com.